# Croydon Libraries

You are welcome to borrow this book for up to 28 days.
If you do not return or renew it by the latest date stamped
below you will be asked to pay overdue charges. You may
renew books in person, by phoning 0208 726 6900 or via the
Council's website www.croydon.gov.uk

| | £4 | |
|---|---|---|
| UNIT TO PUR 8/07 | 18 . July 1. S/Aug. | |
| PURLEY LIBRARY | 16 DEC 2010 | |
| 16 FEB 2008 | -3 DEC 2011 | |
| 06 OCT 2008 | 23 AUG 2012 | |
| -7 NOV 2008 | 19 NOV 2012 | |
| -2 FEB 2009 | 13 SEP 2013 | |
| -8 AUG 2009 | | |
| 27 MAR 2010 | | |
| 17 Mg | | |
| J 0 f4 | | |

**CROYDON
COUNCIL**
www.croydon.gov.uk

# TRINNY & SUSANNAH

## THE SURVIVAL GUIDE

### A WOMAN'S SECRET WEAPON FOR GETTING THROUGH THE YEAR

TRINNY WOODALL & SUSANNAH CONSTANTINE

Photography by Robin Matthews

WEIDENFELD & NICOLSON

# CONTENTS

# INTRODUCTION

**It's a given. We have overflowing lives. Our days spill into each other. We juggle work, our homes, our social lives and have to attempt to look good 365 days a year. The children get mis-called Archie or Honey (our dogs) and our poor husbands hardly get a look in they are so far down the food chain of our daily 'routine'. We end up wishing we had 48-hour days and like Margaret Thatcher needed only a sliver of sleep. Then we could pack even MORE in, and become even more crazed. Ring any bells?**

The idea for this book was born from a personal desire to be more organised and not feel overwhelmed by the weight of our days. Right now we both try to process our daily data in list writing. Susannah is known to sit in meetings appearing to be taking notes while in fact her supermarket shop is being listed on a blank 'Wednesday' in her diary. Trinny will make lists of everyone she has to call, thank you letters she has to write, and the latest cosmetic she MUST have. Very organised, but all these wonderful lists are written in a number of beautifully bound notebooks making it a nightmare to remember where she wrote the damned thing. We have independently looked for the perfect formula – a way to collate our lives in an ordered form. Trinny will experiment electronically, extol the merits of her new 'raspberry', then revert to her notebooks. Susannah, being thick on all things computerised, messes with pin and blackboards, fridge magnets and always goes back to desecrating her diary.

It is very obvious to us that the world is screaming for this essential life planner for women. After all, it is us girls who hold the keys to a happy household.

All our previous books have been born from and based upon our years of experience in dressing and talking to countless women. This book is something altogether different. It combines new information and insights into how we cope with our busy lives. It is packed with solutions and numerous methods of streamlining your own life AND your wardrobe. With so many different facets to each day, we all require something that helps keep our heads above water when things become too hectic. This guide will organise the madness into achievable bytes that aren't forgotten and dates that will no longer be missed. It is the ultimate life planner for women wanting it all.

Sound like a high achieving invention? We believe it is because we know that once it is published our own lives will change. There will be places to keep small and easily lost pieces of vital information: children's shoe sizes, term dates, computer passwords, burglar alarm details. There is space for making lists and prompts to remind you, for example, to book a restaurant table for Valentine's Day, summer holidays or an appointment for your next cervical smear. Plus there are our time-saving tips gleaned from mothers, sisters and girlfriends.

We divulge secrets on how we give anxiety-free dinners, create stress-free (for the adults) children's birthday parties and speedily arrange the perfect dinner party table placement. Holidays will no longer be a hassle. From booking them to taking them, we show how we find the best holiday options and keep everyone happy on plane, train and automobile while packing the ideal capsule holiday wardrobe.

Like a mini encyclopaedia, it also covers hangover and cold remedies, meditation techniques, terrifically useful household hints and looks at the options available if you are thinking of cosmetic surgery.

If you've never used the internet before we will hold your hand and show you how life changing using the worldwide web can be. You'll save time and learn to access information you would not have known where to get before. It's your introduction to a new community. We will save you hours of trawling through options as we have chosen the best of the best, and road tested each site for content, navigation, speed and simplicity of design.

The beauty of this beast is that it will become the only nerve centre of our lives. We hope that it will be just as useful to you.

# Useful numbers

| Organisation | Telephone | Website |
|---|---|---|
| Fire, Police, Ambulance | 999 or 112 | |
| NHS Direct – medical advice | 0845 46 47 | www.nhsdirect.nhs.uk |
| Gas Emergencies – Transco | 0800 111 999 | |
| National Rail Enquiries | 08457 48 49 50 | www.nationalrail.co.uk |
| AA Roadwatch | 09003 401 100 or 401 100 from your mobile. | www.theaa.com/travel |
| Alcoholics Anonymous (AA) Self-help for drink problems | 0845 769 7555 | www.alcoholics-anonymous.org.uk |
| Drinkline | 0800 917 8282 | |
| Al-Anon – Self-help for families and friends of alcoholics | 020 7403 0888 | www.al-anonuk.org.uk |
| Narcotics Anonymous (NA) Self-help for drug users | 0845 373 3366 | www.ukna.org |
| Talk to Frank – drugs helpline | 0800 77 66 00 | www.talktofrank.com |
| Families Anonymous (FA) Self-help for families and friends of drug users | 0845 1200 660 | www.famanon.org.uk |
| Debtors Anonymous (DA) Self-help for debt and money issues | 020 7644 5070 | www.debtorsanonymous.org.uk |
| National Debtline | 0808 808 4000 | www.nationaldebtline.co.uk |
| Samaritans | 08457 90 90 90 | www.samaritans.org.uk |
| Depression Alliance | 0845 123 2320 | www.depressionalliance.org |
| Saneline | 0345 678 000 | www.sane.org.uk |
| NSPCC child protection line | 0808 800 5000 | www.worriedneed2talk.org.uk |
| Childline | 0800 1111 | www.childline.org.uk |
| Parentline Plus. Support for parents | 0808 800 2222 | www.parentlineplus.org.uk |
| National Domestic Violence Helpline | 0808 2000 247 | www.refuge.org.uk |
| Sex and Love Addicts Anonymous (SLAA) Self-help for sex and relationship addiction | 07951 815 087 | www.slaauk.com |
| Overeaters Anonymous (OA) Self-help for eating disorders and food addiction | 07000 784 985 | www.oa.org |
| Gamblers Anonymous (GA) Self-help for gambling addiction | 08700 50 88 80 | www.gamblersanonymous.org.uk |
| Cruse Bereavement Care | 0870 167 1677 | www.crusebereavementcare.org.uk |

# Personal numbers

| Details | Telephone number |
|---|---|
| GP | |
| GP out of hours service | |
| Dentist | |
| Electricity company – emergencies | |
| Water company – emergencies | |
| Electrician | |
| Plumber | |
| Local Police Station | |
| Breakdown service | |
| Mechanic | |
| Local Council | |
| Local Council – Environmental Health | |
| Citizens Advice Bureau | |
| Bank | |
| Bank | |
| Hairdresser | |
| Therapist | |
| Therapist | |
| Vet | |
| School | |
| School | |
| Take away / food delivery | |
| Take away / food delivery | |
| Take away / food delivery | |
| Restaurant | |
| Restaurant | |
| Restaurant | |
| Household insurance | |
| Car insurance | |
| Telephone company | |
| Internet service provider | |
| TV / cable / satellite provider | |

# Important dates

|  | Spring term | Summer term | Autumn term |
|---|---|---|---|
| Start |  |  |  |
| Half-term |  |  |  |
| End |  |  |  |
| Start |  |  |  |
| Half-term |  |  |  |
| End |  |  |  |

# Holidays and anniversaries

| Details | Date | Notes |
|---|---|---|
|  |  |  |
|  |  |  |
|  |  |  |
|  |  |  |
|  |  |  |
|  |  |  |
|  |  |  |
|  |  |  |
|  |  |  |

# Major events

| Details | Date | Notes |
|---|---|---|
|  |  |  |
|  |  |  |
|  |  |  |
|  |  |  |
|  |  |  |
|  |  |  |
|  |  |  |
|  |  |  |
|  |  |  |

# Birthday planner

| | Name | Date | Age | Gift ideas |
|---|---|---|---|---|
| January | | | | |
| February | | | | |
| March | | | | |
| April | | | | |
| May | | | | |
| June | | | | |
| July | | | | |
| August | | | | |
| September | | | | |
| October | | | | |
| November | | | | |
| December | | | | |

# Holidays and celebrations

| | Why it's important | When this year |
|---|---|---|
| New Year's Day | Secular holiday marking the start of a new year. | 1 January |
| Burns Night | Celebrating the birthday of Scottish poet Robert Burns. Readings of his works accompany a feast of haggis and Scottish fare. | 25 January |
| Australia Day | Celebration of Australian culture marking the landing of Captain Arthur Phillip at Sydney Cove in 1788. | 26 January |
| Chinese New Year | Based on the complicated Chinese calendar, it usually falls in late January or early February. This is a 15-day festival for Chinese people of all religions marked by family reunions and remembrance of the deceased. | |
| St Valentine's Day | Celebration of romantic love. | 14 February |
| Shrove Tuesday (Pancake day) | Pancakes are made to use up all the cream, milk and fat on the last Tuesday before Lent begins. | |
| Ash Wednesday | Lent begins 40 days before Easter day (not counting Sundays). A period marked by a disciplined diet and spiritual contemplation. | |
| Vernal equinox | Spring is welcomed. | 21 March |
| Passover | Celebration of the exodus of the Jews from Egypt. | |
| Easter | Christian. Commemorating the crucifixion, on Good Friday, and resurrection, on Easter day, of Jesus Christ. Easter day falls on the first full moon after 21 March (the vernal equinox). | |
| May Day | May Day (1 May) is celebrated with a bank holiday on the first Monday in May. | |
| Vesak (Buddha Day) | Prayers and feasting celebrate the birth, enlightenment and death of the Buddha on the first full moon in May. | |
| Spring bank holiday (Whitsun) | Whitsun falls on the seventh Sunday after Easter and celebrates the founding of the Christian Church by the disciples of Jesus. The bank holiday is on the last Monday in May. | |
| Summer solstice | Celebration of midsummer's day. | 21 June |
| American Independence Day | Celebrating the defeat of the British in 1776 and America's Declaration of Independence. | 4 July |
| Bastille Day | Celebrating the storming of the Bastille and the fall of the French monarchy in 1789. | 14 July |

| | Why it's important | When this year |
|---|---|---|
| Summer bank holiday | Last Monday in August (England, Wales and N. Ireland). First Monday in August (Scotland). | |
| Rosh HaShanah | Jewish New Year celebrated on the day of the new moon at the beginning of the Hebrew Year. | |
| Autumnal equinox | Observing the change of the seasons. | 21 September |
| Diwali | Hindu New Year 5-day 'Festival of Light', also celebrated by Sikhs. Usually falls in October or November. | |
| Yom Kippur | Holiest day of the Jewish year. Observed with strict fasting. Falls on the tenth day of the New Year. | |
| Ramadan | Calculated by the Islamic lunar calendar, Ramadan starts 11 days earlier each year. Marked by fasting from sunrise to sunset and reading one-thirtieth of the Koran each day for thirty days. Working hours are reduced. | |
| Eid-al-Fitr | Immediately following Ramadan, Eid-al-Fitr is a major holiday celebrated with prayers, gifts and a big meal. The exact day of the celebration is not known until the evening before. | |
| Halloween (All Souls' Day) | Originally an ancient Celtic harvest festival. Now a mish-mash of Pagan, Christian and secular celebrations. Children dress up as ghouls and witches to exhort all things spooky. | 31 October |
| Bonfire night | The Gunpowder Plot of 1605 is remembered with ceremonial burnings of Guy Fawkes (guys) on bonfires and firework displays. | 5 November |
| Thanksgiving (USA) | Fourth Thursday in November. American families reunite over a big meal. | |
| Hannukah | Commemorating the rededication of the Temple in Jerusalem in 165BC. Usually falls in December or late November. | |
| Winter solstice | The shortest day of the year | 21 December |
| Christmas | Christian celebration of the birth of Jesus Christ. | 25 December |
| Eid ul-Adha | The most important feast of Islam concluding the Hajj. A 3-day festival recalling Abraham's willingness to sacrifice his son in obedience to Allah. | |
| Hogmanay / New Year's Eve | The last day of the year is celebrated with wild partying. All strangers are welcomed with a kiss and Robert Burns' 'Auld Lang Syne' is sung at midnight. | 31 December |

With thanks to www.interfaithcalendar.org

# Size conversion charts

## Women

| | BRITAIN IRELAND | FRANCE SPAIN PORTUGAL BELGIUM | ITALY | GERMANY AUSTRIA NETHERLANDS SWITZERLAND SWEDEN | USA, CANADA | JAPAN | AUSTRALIA NEW ZEALAND |
|---|---|---|---|---|---|---|---|
| **Dresses** | 6 | 34 | 38 | 32 | 2 | 7 | 8 |
| | 8 | 36 | 40 | 34 | 4 | 9 | 10 |
| | 10 | 38 | 42 | 36 | 6 | 11 | 12 |
| | 12 | 40 | 44 | 38 | 8 | 13 | 14 |
| | 14 | 42 | 46 | 40 | 10 | 15 | 16 |
| | 16 | 44 | 48 | 42 | 12 | 17 | 18 |
| | 18 | 46 | 50 | 44 | 14 | 19 | 20 |
| | 20 | 48 | 52 | 46 | 16 | 21 | 22 |
| **Bra** | 30 | 80 | 0 | 65 | 30 | 65 | 8 |
| | 32 | 85 | 1 | 70 | 32 | 70 | 10 |
| | 34 | 90 | 2 | 75 | 34 | 75 | 12 |
| | 36 | 95 | 3 | 80 | 36 | 80 | 14 |
| | 38 | 100 | 4 | 85 | 38 | 85 | 16 |
| | 40 | 105 | 5 | 90 | 40 | 90 | 18 |
| | 42 | 110 | 6 | 95 | 42 | 95 | 20 |
| **Cup size** | A | A | A | A | AA | A | AA |
| | B | B | B | B | A | B | A |
| | C | C | C | C | B | C | B |
| | D | D | D | D | C | D | C |
| | DD | E | E | E | D | E | D |
| | E | F | F | F | DD | F | DD |
| | F | G | G | G | DDD | G | E |
| | G | H | H | H | F | H | F |
| | H | I | I | I | G | I | G |
| | I | J | J | J | H | J | H |
| | J | K | K | K | I | K | I |
| **Shoes** | 2 | 35 | 35 | 35 | 4.5 | 21 | 4.5 |
| | 3 | 36 | 36 | 36 | 5 | 22 | 5 |
| | 4 | 37 | 37 | 37 | 6 | 23 | 6 |
| | 5 | 38 | 38 | 38 | 7 | 24 | 7 |
| | 6 | 39 | 39 | 39 | 8 | 25 | 8 |
| | 7 | 40 | 40 | 40 | 9 | 26 | 9 |
| | 8 | 41 | 41 | 41 | 10 | 27 | 10 |
| | 9 | 42 | 42 | 42 | 10.5 | 28 | 10.5 |

## Waist sizes for jeans

| INCHES | 24" | 25" | 26" | 27" | 28" | 29" | 30" | 31" | 32" | 33" | 34" | 35" | 36" | 37" | 38" | 39" | 40" |
|---|---|---|---|---|---|---|---|---|---|---|---|---|---|---|---|---|---|
| CM | 61 | 63 | 66 | 69 | 71 | 74 | 76 | 79 | 81 | 84 | 86 | 89 | 91 | 94 | 96 | 99 | 101 |

## men

**Men's shirts**

| BRITAIN<br>IRELAND<br>USA<br>CANADA<br>INCHES | EUROPE<br>JAPAN<br>CM |
|---|---|
| 14" | 36 |
| 14.5" | 37 |
| 15" | 38 |
| 15.5" | 39 |
| 16" | 41 |
| 16.5" | 42 |
| 17" | 43 |
| 17.5" | 44 |
| 18" | 45 |

**Jacket**

| BRITAIN<br>IRELAND<br>USA | EUROPE |
|---|---|
| 36 | 46 |
| 38 | 48 |
| 40 | 50 |
| 42 | 52 |
| 44 | 54 |
| 46 | 56 |

## children

**Shoes**

| BRITAIN<br>IRELAND | EUROPE | USA |
|---|---|---|
| Infant 3 | 19 | 3.5 |
| Infant 4 | 21 | 5 |
| Infant 5 | 22 | 5.5 |
| Infant 6 | 23 | 6.5 |
| Infant 7 | 24 | 7.5 |
| Infant 8 | 25 | 8.5 |
| Infant 9 | 27 | 9.5 |
| Infant 10 | 28 | 10.5 |
| Infant 11 | 29 | 11.5 |
| Infant 12 | 31 | 12.5 |
| Infant 13 | 32 | 13.5 |
| Adult 1 | 33 | 1.5 |
| Adult 2 | 34 | 2.5 |
| Adult 3 | 36 | 3.5 |

# Family sizes

## women

| NAME | BRA | DRESS | TOP | SKIRT/<br>TROUSERS | JEANS | INSIDE LEG | SHOE |
|---|---|---|---|---|---|---|---|
|  |  |  |  |  |  |  |  |
|  |  |  |  |  |  |  |  |
|  |  |  |  |  |  |  |  |
|  |  |  |  |  |  |  |  |
|  |  |  |  |  |  |  |  |

## men

| NAME | SHIRT | JACKET | TROUSER | INSIDE LEG | SHOE |
|---|---|---|---|---|---|
|  |  |  |  |  |  |
|  |  |  |  |  |  |
|  |  |  |  |  |  |
|  |  |  |  |  |  |
|  |  |  |  |  |  |

## children

| NAME | AGE | HEIGHT | WEIGHT | SHOE SIZE |
|---|---|---|---|---|
|  |  |  |  |  |
|  |  |  |  |  |
|  |  |  |  |  |
|  |  |  |  |  |
|  |  |  |  |  |

January

|  | Get to the sales |  |  |
|---|---|---|---|
| 1 | 2 | 3 | 4 |
| 9 | 10 | 11 | 12 |
| Think about booking a weekend break | | | Treat yourself to a pedicure |
| 17 | 18 | 19 | 20 |
| 25 | 26 | 27 | 28 |

# JANUARY

| | | | |
|---|---|---|---|
| 5 | Make sure the tree and all decorations are down<br><br>6 | 7 | 8 |
| Sell unwanted Christmas presents on eBay<br><br>13 | 14 | 15 | 16 |
| 21 | 22 | 23 | 24 |
| Revisit sales for last-minute bargains<br><br>29 | 30 | Book a restaurant for Valentine's Day<br><br>31 | |

'Feeling broke, but need a fix? Arrange a clothes swapping party with your girlfriends...and exchange unwanted gifts at the same time.'

# HOW TO SHOP

## The Ten Commandments of shopping

### 1

**DO**

At the beginning of each season go through your wardrobe and make a list of what you are lacking. Keep it in your handbag at all times. This will help you to focus on what you really need when shopping.

**DON'T**

Go browsing in the shops every time you have a few spare moments. You will end up buying impulsively, spending more than you can afford on things that you don't need and getting into debt.

### 2

**DO**

Know the rules for dressing your body shape and which colours suit you. This will enable you to skim the rails in each shop, find something that suits you and avoid items that don't. You will enter the changing rooms with six items that will work as opposed to a depressing number that will not.

**DON'T**

Take endless items into the changing room in the wrong shapes and colours for you, just because you like the way they look in the shop window.

### 3

**DO**

Set yourself a budget for the day and stick to it.

**DON'T**

Overspend recklessly. If you are drawn to something that is beyond your budget ask yourself how many times you would wear it in a year and then work out the cost per wear. Think about it overnight, it will still be there tomorrow. If it isn't, then it was never meant to be yours.

### 4

**DO**

Take an objective friend who will tell you the truth about what suits you.

**DON'T**

Ask the sales person their opinion. Their job is to flatter your ego and get your cash.

### 5

**DO**

Take a break for lunch, but don't eat anything that bloats you.

**DON'T**

Shop when you are really hungry. You will make wild and needy choices. Shopping on a fat day will leave you with bags of disappointment and no clothes.

**6**

### DO
Make a planned shopping trip when you have time to go at a relaxed pace.

### DON'T
Fly into the nearest store in a panic because you HAVE to have a new dress for your big date this evening.

**7**

### DO
Decide beforehand which stores you will visit and how much time you have to shop. Set the alarm on your mobile phone to ring 15 minutes before your parking meter runs out.

### DON'T
Wander aimlessly from rail to rail. If you have been in any one shop for more than an hour you need to get outside and re-evaluate what you are doing.

**8**

### DO
Try internet shopping. You can buy nearly everything available from the high street without the hassle of finding a parking space and jostling with the queues.

### DON'T
Become addicted – you might be in danger of spending more than you realise as you are not pulled down with the physical labours of a shopping expedition.

**9**

### DO
Consider buying your accessories first, as a simple belt can update an old dress or coat and will cost you far less.

### DON'T
Blow your budget with a splurge item that you might only wear twice a year, especially if you are still lacking tons of basics.

**10**

### DO
Experiment with trying on designer labels. Even if you cannot afford that fabulous jacket, there will be a high street version along very soon and it's a great way to get a new take on what suits you in very comfortable surroundings.

### DON'T
Feel intimidated by sales assistants in expensive designer stores. Remember they have their job to do and that you are the customer.

## THE LAST DAY

On the last day of the sale go back and visit the designer sections. You will be amazed at the gems still on offer at slashed prices. Remember to avoid the one-season wonders, even if they're 80% off.

## SHOES GO FAST

Snap them up early, especially if your feet are of average size.

# THE ART OF SALE SHOPPING

## Choose in advance

Go to your favourite department store a few days before the day of the sale armed with a list of things you really need. Try them on then, before the rush of the sale begins. Then on the day the sale starts, arrive early and track down those items you spied out in advance. You won't have to spend hours queueing at the changing rooms, just pop them in your basket and proceed straight to the till.

# WHAT I WANT IN THE SALES:

COLOUR       TO GO WITH

Top

Skirt

Trousers

Jacket/coat

Dress

Shoes

Accessories

Other

'I always go through my
wardrobe before I go sales
shopping so that I know
exactly what I need.'

# BEST

- Belts
- Cashmere
- China
- Crockery
- Cutlery
- Evening dresses
- Gloves
- Hair-care products
- Handbags
- Luggage
- Make-up
- Scented candles
- Soaps
- Socks
- Tights
- Umbrellas
- Underwear

# WORST

Last season's most fashionable item.

Shoes that don't fit you – just for the sake of the label.

Hats – because you never know when you might have to rush off to Ascot.

Anything to which you attach the words 'this might come in handy one day'.

An item in a colour that makes you look like you just threw up.

Anything damaged – it will always feel second best.

Things that might fit you when you have lost weight.

# SUCCESSFUL SHOPPING WITH A TEENAGER

## Tricks for teenage shopping trips

Our daughters are still a long way off teenagerdom, so we have yet to discover first hand the joys of wrenching their precociously fashion-conscious mitts away from inappropriate garb. We have plenty of friends however who are constantly battling with their teenage daughter's desire to dress like some ghastly premenstrual pop princess.

**Pay with cash**
Counting out readies at the cashier's till will reinforce her understanding of the cost of clothing.

On the lipstick:

MAKE-UP

**Go for a lip-gloss and concealer from a big name brand. It may be more expensive but the excitement of a Lancôme Juicy Tube will keep her eye off the ice-blue eyeshadows and red lipsticks.**

### Set your boundaries

Make list of what she can buy and fix a budget prior to leaving the house.

### Skirt lengths

If this is contentious, agree in advance the point above which the hem can't go.

### Know where you're going

If you are planning to visit a big department store, get the lie of the land in advance so you can breezily steer away from naughty underwear and pricey designer labels.

### Go big on accessories

It will be something new which can update more than one outfit.

### Mini skirts

If mini skirts are a no-no, then have an alternative up your sleeve. Coloured (not black – too sexy) fishnets or lacy tights are a fabulous diversion that will make her feel grown up.

### Killer heels

If she is killing you for killer heels, compromise with a pair of lower wedges.

On the tube:

LANCÔME
PARIS

JUICY TUBES

Gloss Lèvres
Ultra Brillant
Lip Gloss
Ultra Shiny

# Insider's guide to High Street shops

| Shop | Size range | Need to know | Telephone |
| --- | --- | --- | --- |
| Accessorize | Accessories<br>Shoes 4–8 | The best kept secret is their swimwear. Always drop by when you're at the airport. | 0871 412 9000 |
| Claire's Accessories | Accessories only | Teen paradise for cheap trinkets. Be careful you don't buy so many goodies that you end up looking like a wannabee schoolgirl. | 0121 682 8000 |
| Clarks | Shoes 3–8 half sizes, and size 9 available in some styles. | Wide fittings in the K range and wide leg fittings in some boot styles. | 08705 785 886 |
| Coast | 8–16 | A few stand-alone stores and many concessions in department stores around the UK. Great for coats and evening wear. | 01865 881 986 |
| Dorothy Perkins | 8–22, 8–20 in the Petite and Maternity ranges. Lingerie 34A–38D | Not always well made, but each season will produce ten great buys. | 0845 121 4515 |
| Evans | 16–32<br>Lingerie 38B–50H<br>Shoes 4–10 | Specialising in sizes for big girls. They have tall and petite ranges as well as offering wide-fitting shoes and wider calf legs on boots. There is also an in-store bra measuring and fitting service. Sadly their designs tend to be quite safe and a bit dull. | 0845 121 4514 |
| Faith | Shoes 3–8 (size 9 in a few styles) | Visit once a month to be sure of snapping up the latest amazing styles. Their 'catwalk inspired' range is Faith Solo. | 0800 289 297 |
| Gap | 4–18 | Great for useful basics but ultimately all a bit samey and bland colours. | 0800 427 789 |
| George at ASDA | Main range 8–24. G21 range 6–18. All sizes available in all stores. | We sometimes go seasons without finding much and then they have 20 great buys in one season. Worth checking out and fabulous prices. | 0500 100 055 |
| H&M | 8–16, a few pieces go up to 20 Big is Beautiful 16–30 | Shockingly inattentive staff. Presentation of rails has the air of a jumble sale. On Saturdays we need a flamethrower to get through the crowds. But here we find the most fab dresses, trousers, jacket, T-shirts and accessories and most are under £29.99. | 020 7323 2211 |

# Insider's guide to High Street shops

| Shop | Size range | Need to know | Telephone |
|---|---|---|---|
| Hobbs | Shoes 3–9, half sizes available Clothes 8–16 | We always recommend their great flat boots with a sturdy two-inch heel which go over most chunky calves and make all lower legs look extremely skinny. | 020 7586 5550 |
| Jigsaw | 8–16 (some styles only go up to 14) | The staff are second to none for thoughtful and polite service. Very flattering cuts for disguising flab in unwanted places. Stores are immaculate and everything well presented. | 020 8392 5600 |
| Karen Millen | 8–14 | Don't be put off by the Footballers' Wives image. The clothes come to life when you put them on. | 0870 160 1830 |
| Mango | S–XL | Sizing for anorexics but some funky young looks. | 020 7434 3694 |
| Marks & Spencer | Main range 8–22 Petite 6–22 Plus 20–28 Limited Collection 8–18 8–22 in most lingerie ranges 32A–38 in all bras going up to 40DD in their *Body* range M&S also do a DD–G range. | Famous for their high quality and 'no questions asked' returns police. The standard bearer for quality underwear and bras for every woman. Always worth checking out their leather goods and shoes. Lots of different clothing ranges spread through the store can leave us a bit confused about where to look for a particular garment. Of all the high street chains, M&S seem to be making the most genuine effort to stock goods that are ethically and environmentally responsible. Bras are available in larger sizes. | 0845 302 1234 |
| Matalan | 10–20 (some styles in 8 & 22) Rogers & Rogers range in selected stores 18–28 | Jeff & Co range designed by Jeff Banks is available in some stores. | 0845 330 3330 |
| Monsoon | 8–18 (up to size 22 in a few styles) | Still tend towards a heavy emphasis on the ethnic influences. | 0870 412 9000 |
| New Look | 8–18 Inspire' plus-size range 16–28 | The accessories here are particularly fab. We seem to use them constantly in our column in the *Sun*. Summer seasons are usually stronger than winter ones because while the styles are amazing, the cut in tailoring can occasionally look a little cheap and of course there are naturally more tailored items for the colder months. | 0500 454 094 |

# Insider's guide to High Street shops

| Shop | Size range | Need to know | Telephone |
|------|-----------|--------------|-----------|
| Nine West | 3–8 | The shoes here look really expensive for their price. The sandals give Gina a run for their money and they always have a brilliant selection of fun vibrant colours. | 020 7079 7586 |
| Oasis | 8–16 | Designs seem to have lost their flair lately Gorgeous underwear. Check out their Future Organic range using denim and jersey made from 100% organic cotton. | 01865 881 986 |
| Office | 3–8 | Great shoes for every occasion. Music in-store is deafening. The hottest styles sell out instantly. Office Vintage is a range of retro-inspired funky looks and it is probably the best place to get Converse trainers. | 020 7255 2410 |
| Primark | 8–18 | Shockingly quick at producing great versions of the latest trends. Clothes are so cheap it seems rude not to buy 20 hot items at a time. Don't expect them to last long though. Be prepared to queue for half an hour at the changing room and another half an hour at the till. | 0118 9606 300 |
| Principles | 8–20, Petite 6–16 | Can make surprisingly well-cut clothes. Not as classical as they used to be. Some great shapes for big boobs. | 0870 122 8802 |
| Schuh | 3–8, 9 in a few stores | Great for funky trainers. Look past the rather bland black chunky office shoes and tacky stilettos to find a few true gems including the gorgeous DHavz by Terry de Havilland | 0845 307 2484 |
| Shelly's | 3–8, 9 in selected styles | If you want the best range of cutting edge styles, look no further. You will need to navigate the plethora of cheap and nasty, but boy do they come out with some winning designs. Go early as it gets busier to the point of madness as the day goes by. | 01274 893 886 |
| Tesco | 8–20 Sizes 16–26 in the SIXTEENTWENTYSIX range available in some stores Shoes 3–8 | The great items featured in the magazines are infuriatingly difficult to find in-store. Having said that, the Florence + Fred collection is always worth a look. They do great little waisted jackets. Cherokee is the more casual sporty range. The underwear section is ok but only for very basic cotton pants. | 0800 50 55 55 |

# Insider's guide to High Street shops

| Shop | Size range | Need to know | Telephone |
|---|---|---|---|
| TK Maxx | All designer garments are arranged by size, so no need to waste time browsing clothes that won't fit. It depends on the label, but a good range of sizes across the board. | Sell designer gear at discount prices. It's a bun fight to find the jewels among the thicket of designer rejects but worth it when you dig up an amazing bargain treasure. Great stuff sells out fast but you can stay ahead of the crowd by subscribing to their email newsletter. Something for everybody. | 01923 473 561 |
| Topshop | 6–16 | Don't go on the weekend unless you want to feel totally old and fat. Lead the way in commissioning top designers to produce an own label range. Offer some fabulous services to take the stress out of shopping: Style Advisor (a personal shopper to help you in the store); To Go (they come round to your house with tons of stuff for you to try – this is great for parties!); Express (broken a heel? emergency dinner date? fashion crisis? – they bring 5 garments over immediately for you to try) and Style Alert (text what you desperately want to a style advisor and they will hold it for you). This is groundbreaking service, we hope that the other high street chains will keep up. | 0845 1214 519 |
| Wallis | 8–20, also Petite 8–20 | We have found very well-cut trousers for over size 12s and a number of trouser suits and evening outfits that will add a sense of glam to a 40-somethingish wardrobe. They also always have the best tops for big tits and flabby tummies. | 0845 121 4520 |
| Warehouse | 8–16, size 6 in a few styles | The stores do need a total overhaul and the rails always feel over stacked, but there are occasional good buys if you have the patience to find them. A great range of accessories. | 0870 122 8813 |
| Zara | 6–18 Some styles are not available in the whole size range | Great versions of high-end designer looks. Generously long trouser legs. Labels are sewn on with irritatingly scratchy nylon wire. Mainly Spanish staff are exceptionally helpful. Generally they take an interest in customer comments and feed it back to be taken on board by the design team. We shop here more than any other high street store. | 020 7534 9500 |

# TOPS THE RULES

## Big tits

Deep V lifts and
separates boobs.

Scoop neck shows off
good flesh. Detail around
neckline detracts from
size of tits.

## No waist

Diagonal stripes break
up width while wrap
pulls in the waist.

Horizontal stripes create
optical illusion of a waist.

## Big arms

Batwing sleeves
and pattern balance
out size of arms.

A fluted sleeve ending below
the fattest part of the arms
disguises their size.

# Long body

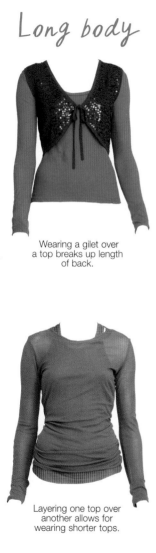

Wearing a gilet over
a top breaks up length
of back.

Layering one top over
another allows for
wearing shorter tops.

# No tits

Ruching around boobs
diverts attention from
lack of breasts.

Showing off a good
back is a sexy alternative
to a cleavage.

# Big tummy

The knot-front top creates folds to
disguise bumps.

Emphasising the narrowness
under the boob line distracts
the eye from the tummy.

| | | | |
|---|---|---|---|
| Think about what to do for half term | | | |
| 1 | 2 | 3 | 4 |
| | Book an Easter break | | |
| 9 | 10 | 11 | 12 |
| | | Get your highlights done for Spring | |
| 17 | 18 | 19 | 20 |
| | If you're going abroad for Christmas, book now! | | |
| 25 | 26 | 27 | 28 |

# FEBRUARY

| | | | |
|---|---|---|---|
| 5<br><br>Send Valentine's<br>cards | 6 | 7 | 8 |
| 13 | 14 | 15<br><br>Check the batteries in<br>your smoke detector | 16 |
| 21 | 22 | 23 | 24 |

'Be organised. Order your
foreign currencies at your
local bank or the post
office instead of being
ripped off at the airport.'

# OUR FAVOURITE
# SHOPPING
# DESTINATIONS

## Some hints for when you are away

**Buy the foreign magazine before you leave on your trip. This will save shopping time by figuring out what you want to buy in advance.**

It's fun to wear the local look when you are abroad but remember that the costume might not travel well and you will probably look like you are in fancy dress when you get home.

**To save rows, do a recce of the shops on your own before you take your partner with you. He will be so impressed by how quick you are that he might even want to pay for something.**

When sleeping under an unknown roof take ear-plugs and an eye-mask. You never know how noisy or light your room might be.

**Think of something you can collect on your travels for your children, be it foreign dolls, lanterns, teacups or snow-globes. It gives them an interest and is still a treat.**

Always try to buy a Christmas decoration at your destination. It is so lovely to have a Christmas tree full of memories.

**Avoid wearing boots to the airport. You will inevitably be asked to remove them at some stage in the security process.**

If you are a business woman staying in a hotel, always remember some good mufty gear like a pair of yoga pants to put on as soon as you get to your hotel room after a long day.

**There is nothing like a weekend break in a foreign city.** There is something naughty and sexy about waking up in a strange place with unfamiliar police and ambulance sirens echoing down exotically named streets. A long weekend is ideal for urban trips. Any longer and we want to go somewhere further afield or as far away from a city as possible. Escaping life is something we try to do at least twice a year. The bliss of child-free meandering around one of our favourite cities recharges our batteries and empties our bank accounts like nothing else. Naturally we are always on the look out for things to buy...little treasures that can't be found back home. Over the years we have collated a list of special shops and restaurants that we love to visit.

# VENICE

If there is one place we love in equal measure, it is Venice, the city with a high romantic expectation that never fails to be met. Even after countless visits, that first sight of Venice upon leaving the airport takes your breath away. It seems almost unfair that a place of such exquisiteness should also hold some of our favourite shops. It is not an obvious shopping Mecca, thus it has taken many trips for us to unearth the retail gems hidden down its watery streets.

## Women's clothes

In Venice you will find all the international designer labels like Bottega Veneta, Fendi, Missoni, Prada and Etro, often with a wider choice and at a better price than in the UK.

### La Coupole
Calle XXII Marzo, san Marco. Tel: +39 041 522 5147
Don't be put off by the façade of this store with its flashy accessories and overdressed mannequins. Among the overpriced and ill-bought labels are some gems by Allessando dell'Acqua, great tops for big boobs and funky accessories you will be hard pushed to find elsewhere.

### United Colours of Benetton
50-51 mercerie 2 Aprile, san Marco. Tel: +39 041 296 0493
Not a natural favourite of ours, but this Venetian outlet prides itself in a wonderfully array of cotton/cashmere mix sweaters. Great for an unexpected cold snap.

## Shoes

### Hogan
Campo san Moisé, san Marco 1461. Tel: +39 041 522 5638
Here you will find the most ingenious, swanky trainers complete with hidden two-inch lift in the heel. Add these inches to your leg while looking like you are loafing around in flats. Oh and by the way, they do them for men too.

## Bags

### Mazzon le Borse
Campiello san Toma 2807. Tel: 1 +39 041 520 3421
We were in two minds as to whether we should mention this shop for fear that an increased popularity might jack up the prices. It specialises in making up classic leather bags in any colour your heart desires. Shapes like the famous Birkin can be yours in the colour of your choice for as little as 260 euros as opposed to a whopping £4000. The boys, too, can benefit from the joy of a bargain when they see the gorgeous belts for 25 euros and fine selection of beautifully crafted briefcases. The bespoke leather goods take about 4 weeks to be delivered. Be aware that little English is spoken, apart from the day you might get the owner's daughter.

## Jewellery

### Paropamiso
Frezzeria 1701, san Marco. Tel: +39 041 522 7120
Paropamiso specializes in unique European and oriental antique jewellery. Trinny's two favourite necklaces came from here. It has exquisite pieces that will make a manhole in your bank account.

### Rialta
Sottoportici di Rialto 56. Tel: +39 041 528 5710
Imagine Butler and Wilson on drugs and you get Rialta. This is where you find earrings and necklaces that people will assume you have released from a bank vault for the night. Exquisite paste jewellery designed by the master of the fakes. Prices from 30 euros.

### Gloria Astolfo
Frezzeria san Marco 1581. Tel: +39 041 520 6827
You will find a limited selection of Gloria's designs at Catherine Prevost in London, but her Venice store will satisfy the most ardent fan of her glittering gems. She uses Murano glass and lots of semi-precious stones. A scene-stealing pair of earrings will set you back 50 euros.

## Hair

### Marie Rose
San Marco 2465. Tel: +39 041 522 5374
Andreas and his sister Marie Rose have had the salon for 30 years. When in need of a cut or blow dry we go nowhere else and are always delighted with the results. They also will do weddings and special occasions. Closed Sunday and Monday.

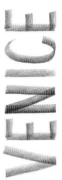

## Men's clothes
### Black Watch
Calle del Forno, san Marco 4594. Tel: +39 041 523 1945
The Egyptian cotton shirts at 120 euros were a real find for our husbands. They also stock the most divine if pricey cashmere jackets by Zikon, and the classic Italian 'slack' in every conceivable colour. Mainly for the conservative man who occasionally steps out of his comfort zone.

## Kids
### Il Nido delle Cicogne
Campo san Toma 2806. Tel: +39 041 528 7497
Ignore the Burberry stuff and look out for the number of very pretty Italian labels for classic girls dresses and endless boxes of exquisite baby clothes.

### Kappa Venezia
Ponte di Rialto, san Polo 12/13. Tel: +39 041 522 5638
There is no better gift for a football-crazed child (or adult for that matter) than a personalised strip from their favourite team. With a selection of shirts from over 50 European teams, most fans should be catered for.

## Eating while shopping
### Harry's Bar
1323 san Marco 30100. Tel: +39 041 520 8822
The food is not so good any more, but the atmosphere still evokes Venice.

### Harry's Dolce
774 Giudecca 30100. Tel: +39 041 520 8337
Harry's little sister on the Giudecca. The food here is fabulous.
Great for lunch

### Locanda Cipriani
29 Piazza san Fosca. Tel: +39 041 730 150
This is a gorgeous water taxi ride away and has the most beautiful garden setting. Best for al fresco eating.

### Madonna
Calle della Madonna san Polo 594. Tel: +39 041 522 3824
Although the location is very unappealing (stuffed down a back alley with no view), its deliciously simple food is a firm favourite with the locals. You won't feel like a tourist here.

### Da Ivo
San Marco 1809. Tel: +39 41 528 5004
A tiny pixie place that serves the most deliciously simple food. Low key yet dead classy.

# PARIS

**From surreptitious shopping sprees to Trinny's hen night, we've always had wonderful times in Paris. Yes, it's the city of romance, but it's also great for a girly weekend.**

## Women's clothes

**Colette**
213 rue Saint Honoré 75001. Tel: +33 1 55 35 33 90
The hippest mini-department store in town with a great accessories and gadgets department on the ground floor and the largest display of bottled water in the downstairs restaurant.

**Antik Batik**
18 rue de Turenne, 75004. Tel: +33 1 44 47 80 20
Chilled-out wear for the beach and summer holidays – kaftans, dresses and accessories all with an eastern influence. The original sophisticated hippy label.

**Isabel Marant**
1 rue Jacob 75006. Tel: +33 1 43 26 04 12
The darling of Parisian fashion, fabulous clothes and accessories. Her pieces are timeless. Definitely worth popping into.

**APC**
3-4 rue des Fleurus 75006. Tel: +33 1 42 22 12 77
The quintessential of cool, APC has the best accessories as well as great music and fabulous clothes. A cult shop among savvy young Parisians. Classic basics.

**Vanessa Bruno**
12 rue de Castiglione 75001. Tel: +33 1 42 61 44 60
Beautiful shop with the entire VB collection. Well worth a trip.

### Maje
13 rue Aboukir 75002. Tel: +33 1 42 36 26 26
Slightly cheaper version of Vanessa Bruno, affordably chic Parisian dressing.

### Zadig et Voltair
42 rue des Francs Bourgeois 75003. Tel: +33 1 44 54 00 60
A great shop that caters to all chic Parisian girls, they have fabulous fine cashmere jumpers at really great prices.

### Maria Louisa
4 rue Cambon. Tel: +33 1 47 03 48 08
Boutique with European labels. Great buying, the French equivalent of Browns.

### L'Eclaireur
3 rue des Rosiers 75003. Tel: +33 1 48 87 10 22
Very trendy shop with its own label, this shop has a definite following.

### Onward
147bis blvd St Germain 75006. Tel: +33 1 55 42 77 56
High fashion labels for high fashion lovers. Think mini Selfridges.

### Tsumori Chisato
20 rue Barbette 75003. Tel: +33 1 42 78 18 88
Japanese designer with the best tops ever! Seriously fabulous clothes, you must visit this shop.

### Kokon Tozai
48 rue Tiquetonne 75002. Tel: +33 1 42 36 92 41
Uber trendy store. For cutting edge fashion this is the ultimate place to be.

### Martin Margiela
25bis rue de Montpensier 75001. Tel: +33 1 40 15 04 36
Very high fashion, the most beautiful fabrics and tailoring.

### Costume National
5 rue Cambon 1st. Tel: +33 1 40 15 04 36
Very sombre looking shop that is rather intimidating at first. Don't be put off as there are some real timeless classics to be found here.

### Agnès B
2 rue du Jour 7500. Tel: +33 1 40 39 96 88
For French classics. This store never goes out of style.

## Shoes

### Repetto
22 rue de la Paix 75002. Tel: +33 1 44 71 83 00
Great ballet shoes for women. An establishment among Parisians.

### Rodolphe Menudier
14 rue de Castiglione 75001. Tel: +33 1 42 60 86 27
Beautifully sexy shoes in a fabulously decadent environment.

### Pierre Hardy

156 galerie des Valois 75001. Tel: +33 1 42 60 59 75
Shoes that are literally to die for. Set in the Jardins du
Palais Royale, the shop is breathtakingly beautiful, so
much so you'll probably want to move in!

## Swimwear
### Eres

4 rue de Cherche Midi, 75006. Tel: +33 1 47 42 28 82
Without a doubt the best swimwear in the world. Great
shop and the staff are really helpful too.

## Underwear
### Sabia Rosa

73 rue de Saints. Tel: +33 1 45 48 88 37
This shop is like stepping into a boudoir. The most
gorgeous lingerie in so many amazing colours you'll
be overwhelmed!

## Bags
### Jamin Puech

61 rue d'Hauteville, 75010. Tel: +33 1 40 22 08 32
Gorgeous shop that has an amazing vintage feel about it
and the most fantastic bags.

## Department store
### Bon Marché

22 Rue de Sèvres 75006. Tel: +33 1 44 39 80 00
Absolute heaven, all the young up-and-coming labels can be
found here as well as top designers. The contemporary floor
is well worth a visit.

## Kids
### Bonton

82 rue de Grenelle 75007. Tel: +33 1 44 29 09 20
French children are arguably the best dressed on the planet.
This is where all the chic Parisian women shop for their tots.
The most amazing kids' clothes you've ever seen.

### Petit Bateau

26 rue Vavin 75006. Tel: +33 1 55 42 02 53
Classic children's day and nightwear. The size 14 and 16
fit a grown up 8–12.

## Quick eats
### Fauchon

30 place de la Madeleine, 75008. Tel: +33 1 42 65 17 60
From macaroons to cakes, and loads more delicious food.
Part of the establishment.

### Hediard

21 place de la Madeleine 75008. Tel: +33 1 43 12 88 88
Rare teas and coffee, jams and candied fruits. The perfect place
for sweet tooths.

# NEW YORK

**New York is a heck of a way to go for two days but quite manageable and well worth it for a long weekend. Once you've done the Statue of Liberty, been to MOMA and the Met, checked a Broadway show or two, the only thing to do is shop. And, boy, is New York the place for that. We both know this city well so we are happy to share shops we have found well off the beaten track.**

## Women's clothes

**Scoop**
532 Broadway, near Spring Street. Tel: +1 212 925 2886
Six stores around New York They have many British designers sold here but at a much better price. They also do a range of great T-shirts from C&C California and the latest, trendiest jeans.

**Marc Jacobs**
163 Mercer Street. Tel: +1 212 343 1490 (womens clothing)
403 Bleecker Street Tel +1 21 924 0026 (accessories and Marc)
The epitome of New York style with the largest MJ selection.
Look out for the sales, especially of evening dresses.

**Jane Mayle**
242 Elizabeth St (NoLita). Tel: +1 212 625 0406
This English designer produces a range of pretty, feminine, vintage-inspired clothes.

## Tori Burch

257 Elizabeth Street (NoLita). Tel: +1 212 334 3000
A store for 30-somethings who feel they need some trending up but don't want to stray too far from conservatism. The uptown girl's version of a downtown store. Great tops and cashmere, trousers and lots of room for men to lounge around on comfortable sofas as you continue to shop.

## Barney's Co-op

660 Madison Avenue at 61st Street. Tel: +1 212 826 8900
Go for the women's clothing on the 7th and 8th floors where they focus on home-grown US labels of up-and-coming and established less expensive designers. They always have a great sale rack.

## Kirna Zabete

96 Greene Street (SoHo). Tel: +1 212 941 9656
Stocks Gaultier, Balenciaga, and other European and American designers. Great accessories.

## Vintage clothes

### Resurrection

217 Mott Street between Spring and Prince Streets (NoLita).
Tel: +1 212 625 1374
This is probably the most expensive vintage store in New York, but you can guarantee that it will have the best quality merchandise. Trinny picked up an immaculate YSL cashmere cape for $400. It is worth bargaining.

### Cherry

19 8th Avenue, between Jane and W12th Sts (West Village).
Tel: +1 212 924 1410
A trendy selection of vintage clothes, not only designer labels. You will find unique pieces at great prices.

### Edith and Daha

104 Rivington Street. Tel: +1 212 979 9992
This is arguably the best vintage store in New York. Certainly the most unreliable, as it is never guaranteed when it will be actually open, but worth the hassle once you get inside.

### Marmalade

172 Ludlow Street (Lower East Side) Tel +1 212 473 8070
Less expensive, great vintage. Not such well-known labels.

### Frock NYC

148 Orchard Street, between Stanton and Rivington Streets.
Tel: +1 212 594 5380
A well-chosen selection of designer pieces in excellent condition.

## Vintage jewellery

### Pippin

72 Orchard Street (Lower East Side). Tel: +1 212 505 5159
A tiny little shop, named after the owner's dog. They have a constantly changing stock of really interesting and well-priced vintage jewellery sourced from outside New York.

## Shoes
### Jeffrey's
449 West 14th Street (Meatpacking district). Tel: +1 212 206 1272
The best selection of designer shoes in New York with prices to match the swanky names. Thankfully they have a sale twice a year which slashes prices in half.

## Beauty & health
### Bigelow
414 6th Avenue. Tel: +1 212 533 2700
A traditional old-school pharmacy, with a great range of upscale products including Kiehl's and Nars.

### Duane Reed
Stores throughout New York
One of the biggest is 535 5th Avenue at 44th/45th St.
Tel: +1 212 687 8641
The most amazing chemist that looks like an over-populated hardware store. Look out for their miniatures. Toothpaste, deodorant, shampoos and conditioners all come in handy travel sizes. They also have mad things like temporary fillings for teeth and bee sting removers. It may be a humble drug store, but it's a really fun place to browse around.

### Vitamin Shoppe
139 East 57th Street. Tel: +1 212 421 0250
This chain has a number of stores around New York. Go for the 'EmergenC' sachets at half the UK price and Melatonin for jetlag which is no longer sold in the UK, but is still FDA approved. Other vitamins and minerals are far cheaper than in the UK

### Kiehl's
109 Third Avenue, Between 13th & 14th Streets. Tel: +1 212 677 3171
If you want to see the entire range of Kiehl's products you'll need to swing by their original store. Here you will find a glorious selection of potions interspersed with the owner's original motorbike collection (something for the boys). They are very generous with their samples.

## Department stores
### Bergdorf Goodman
754 Fifth Avenue, at 57th Street. Tel: +1 212 753 7300
Avoid the European designer floors and go straight for labels that the Americans term 'sportswear' but turn out to be the likes of Diane von Furstenberg and Theory.

### Henri Bendel
712 5th Avenue. Tel: +1 212 247 1100
There is a fantastic selection of own label cashmere here and in the sales you will find them at under $100. Bendel's is also famous for its brown and white striped wash bags in every shape and size. They carry an excellent selection of US designers housed in a smaller and more manageable space than other department stores on this street. The cosmetic hall is fabulous, despite the over-keen sales staff.

### Century 21
22 Cortlandt Street, between Church & Broadway. Tel: +1 212 227 9092
Although a nightmare, this shopping emporium still holds some real treasures. Head for the Ralph Lauren menswear and upstairs to the

European and American designers like Marc Jacobs, Alberta Feretti, John Galliano, Prada, Miu Miu and Marni The sizing is erratic and the goods can be damaged, but the prices are staggeringly cheap.

## All the family

### Abercrombie & Fitch
693 Fifth Avenue, between 54th and 55th Streets.
Tel: +1 212 350 0100, or 199 Water Street, at Fulton Street
Tel: +1 212 809 9000
A great selection of casual wear with a twist. Teenagers love their signature T-shirts and the men's swimming trunks are dead cool. It's a fab place to send sullen teenagers who are fed up of being dragged around with their parents.

### Dylan's Candy Store
1011 Third Avenue at 60th Street (Midtown).
Tel: +1 646 735 0078
Ralph Lauren's daughter has opened a delightful candy store that will appeal to all ages.

### Target
139 Flatbush Ave, Brooklyn. Tel: +1 718 290 1109
This is the nearest you'll get to M&S in the US. Brilliant for Christmas presents for kids. Designers like Cynthia Rowley or Izaac Mizrahi occasionally produce ranges for Target.

## Gifts

### The Metropolitan Museum Shop
1000 5th Avenue at 82nd Street Tel 1-800 468 7386
For a great selection of arty gifts including repro jewellery from Roman times.

## Home

### Bed, Bath and Beyond
620 6th Avenue (Chelsea) Tel +1 212 255 3550
Fabulous sheets, towels and home wares. Luggage space will probably prevent you going wild, but even with shipping costs savings can be made.

## Feeding while shopping

### Dean & Deluca
560 West Broadway (at Prince). Tel: +1 212 226 6800
Does the BEST cheesecake in the world!

### Gardenia Diner
797 Madison Avenue (67th and 68th Street)
Tel +1 212 628 8763
Your classic diner with a great fattening and delicious menu.

### Katz's Delicatessen
205 E Houston St. Tel: +1 212 254 2246
The yummiest matzo ball soup.

### The Oyster Bar
Grand Central Station. Tel: +1 212 490 6650
No trip to New York is complete without snacking on seafood at this cathedral of oysters.

# LONDON

## Now here is a town we really do know inside out...

### Women's clothes
**Matches**
60-64 Ledbury Road W11. Tel: 020 7221 0255
We always kick off the new season at this
fabulous boutique. Their choice of designers
is a little edgy, very wearable if expensive.
You can have a civilised browse where the
number of labels will educate rather than
confuse. Across the road they have a boutique
with diffusion labels and also own the Diane
von Furstenberg shop. PS: they serve a great
cappuccino to those who know to ask.

**The Cross**
141 Portland Road, W11. Tel: 020 7727 6760
The Cross is the original Notting Hill boutique that introduced many
US labels to the UK. Each season they show another new designer as
well as old favourites like Missoni and Luisa Beccaria. A dazzling
selection of goodies (for children too) and own-label cashmere.

**A La Mode**
10 Symons Street, SW3. Tel: 020 7730 7180
Josephine and David have introduced some wonderful designers to
London, such as Marc Jacobs and Viktor & Rolf. Here you will find some
genuinely unique pieces – old favourites like John Galliano as well as
one or two new designers each season. They also have a great sale.

**Koh Samui**
65 Monmouth Street, WC2. Tel: 020 7240 4280
Always have the latest, chicest items by names like Marc Jacobs and
Missoni, plus a few well-chosen, more avant-garde designer pieces.

**Paradiso**
60 Dean Street and 41 Old Compton Street, W1. Tel: 020 7287 6913
This is the acceptable face of PVC.

**Ross and Bute**
57 Ledbury Road, W11. Tel: 020 7727 7400
Quirky designed clothes for real women. Wonderful satin nighties,
vintage-style dresses and velvet and lace trim cotton tops.

**Mimi**
309 Kings Road, SW3. Tel: 020 7349 9699
The Kings Road version of the Cross in Notting Hill. Lots of labels
to choose from and some very good shoes and bras.

**Coco Ribbon**
133 Sloane Street, SW3. Tel: 020 7730 8555
21 Kensington Park Road, W11. Tel: 020 7229 4904
Eclectic mix of cute girlie stuff from knickers to chandeliers – to die for.

**Dover Street Market**
17–18 Dover Street, W1. Tel: 020 7518 0680
Cross between an art gallery, a factory and an indoor market.
Selected designers all measure at least 9.8 on the fashion Richter Scale

## Cashmere
**Brora**
66 Ledbury Road, W11. Tel: 020 7229 1515
There are five other stores in London. Thick, luxurious cashmere in
great colours and shapes for men, women and children. Great for gifts.

## Underwear
**Bodas**
38b Ledbury Road, W11. Tel: 020 7792 4915
Essential underwear only –beige, white and nude thongs, trouser and
granny knickers and comfortable bras for the average size.

**Agent Provocateur**
6 Broadwick St, W1. Tel: 020 7439 0229
16 Pont Street, SW1. Tel: 020 7235 0229
The original sexy underwear store, a treat for both girls and boys.

**Rigby & Peller**
22a Conduit Street, W1. Tel: 020 7491 2200
2 Hans Road, SW3. Tel: 020 7581 8915
We send every woman who really needs to re-evaluate her bra size and
type here. A huge range of sizes and styles.

**Coco de Mer**
23 Monmouth Street, WC2. Tel: 020 7836 8882
An upmarket sex shop that sells all the usual suspects, but of the
highest quality and in good taste. It's worth going in just for the décor.

## Shoes
**Manolo Blahnik**
49-51 Old Church Street, SW3. Tel: 020 7352 3863
They don't sell shoes, they sell Manolos! An addiction all of its own.

**Christian Louboutin**
23 Motcomb St, SW1. Tel: 020 7245 6510
Consistently our favourite shoes – most flattering for a thicker ankle.

## Vintage
**Rellik**
8 Golborne Road, W10. Tel: 020 8962 0089
££ Stuffed with 20th-century gems from Balenciaga to Westwood.

**Portobello Road market, W11 & W10**
£+ Huge street market. Go on Fridays (under the Westway) for funky vintage, Saturday for antique clothes and jewellery at the Notting Hill end of the road and under the Westway for more modern pieces. Try the Golborne Road flea market if you are really committed.

**Retro Woman**
34 Pembridge Road, W11. Tel: 020 7792 1715
££ The shop feels a bit flea-bitten but there are some good buys and they also do trade-ins.

**One of a Kind**
253 Portobello Road, W11. Tel: 020 7589 2233
£££. Unique designer pieces at unique prices.

## Men's clothes
**Richard James**
29 Savile Row, W1. Tel: 020 7434 0605
Ready-to-wear and made-to-measure suits to bring out the inner James Bond in every bloke.

## Department store
**Selfridges**
400 Oxford Street, W1. Tel: 0870 837 7377
If we had to send a woman to one store in London for clothes without knowing her budget or shape it would always be Selfridges.

## Kids
**Preposterous Presents**
262 Upper Street, N1. Tel: 020 7226 4166
An Aladdin's cave of giant snakes, fake dog-do, itching powder and similar horrible tricks for kids of all ages.

## Gifts
**Cath Kidston**
51 Marylebone High St, W1. Tel: 020 7935 6555
An adorable shop for those who like rose and floral prints in a myriad of items from china and nighties to cushions and children's lamps.

**Nicky Haslam**
12 Holbein Place SW1. Tel: 020 7230 8623
This interior designer shop carries gorgeous accessories for the home. Susannah buys Trinny her most loved birthday presents here.

**Smythson**
40 New Bond Street, W1. Tel: 020 7629 8558
Smythson has come a long way since being the diary at the end of your Christmas stocking. Now they produce a superb range of gifts from passport and jewellery holders to handbags.

**James Smith & Sons**
53 New Oxford Street, WC2. Tel: 020 7836 4731
For a classic or quirky British brolly, Smiths have the finest selection.

### The Tea Palace
175 Westbourne Grove, W11. Tel: 020 7727 2600
What do we give to the person who has everything? Really
expensive tea in an embroidered purple satin bag. This is also a
great place for afternoon tea if you need a break from shopping.

### British Museum Shop
Great Russell Street, WC1. Tel: 020 7323 8000
Presents with an historical twist.

### Connolly
41 Conduit Street W1. Tel: 020 7235 3883
Luxury with a capital L leather goods. Need a calfskin covered,
silver-embossed London A–Z? This is where to get it.

## Books, music and DVDs
### Daunt Books
83 Marylebone High St, W1. Tel: 020 7224 2295
112-114 Holland Park Avenue, W11. Tel: 020 7727 7022
Browse through a really well thought-out selection of books
in this atmospheric old London favourite.

### Fopp
1 Earlham Street, WC2. Tel: 020 7379 0883
Great for stocking up on cult books and films at unbeatable prices.

## Quick eats
### Maroush
38 Beauchamp Place, SW3. Tel: 0871 332 7910
Delicious, healthy Lebanese delicacies and juices.

### Wagamama
101A Wigmore Street, W1. Tel: 020 7409 0111
Asian feeding station for a fast and yummy noodle fix.

### Selfridges Salt Beef Bar
Ground floor, Selfridges 400 Oxford Street, W1. Tel: 020 318 3679
To find better a salt beef sandwich than this you would have to travel
east to Brick Lane or west to New York.

### Fresh & Wild
208-212 Westbourne Grove, W11. Tel: 020 7229 1063
For quick organic food and sublime fresh juices.

### Ottolenghi
63 Ledbury Road, W11. Tel: 020 7727 1121
The most divine snacks this side of Paradise. Sit down at the small
communal table or stock up for a blow-out at home.

### Chinatown
Gerrard and Lisle Streets, W1
Great lunchtime specials like roast duck on rice or dim sum.

### Prêt à Manger
Branches all over London
The freshest salads and most imaginative sarnies can be found here.
And they use only organic milk in their coffee.

# BAGS THE RULES

## Cocktail

The long strap hangs elegantly from the wrist, allowing you to use both hands.

Varied colours are versatile and will go with almost any outfit.

## In-flight

A big soft bag will expand to hold everything from a big shop-up abroad.

Business-like yet flexible enough to contain all your in-flight kit and computer.

## Baby

This is big enough to hold the changing mat and nappies, yet the long strap still allows hands-free movement.

Try out a great beach bag as an alternative to a more cumbersome baby bag. Adapt the pockets to fit bottles of milk and necessary lotions and potions.

# Work

This perennially elegant style takes all the necessities of the modern business woman without resorting to an ugly black holdall.

Consider navy as a more interesting alternative to black

# Long dress

If you have an hourglass figure this curvy clutch bag will compliment your shape.

Jazz up an old bag with a huge brooch as an alternative way to add sparkle to your outfit.

# Casual evening

Use a leather bag in a medium size that can slide snugly under the arm.

Try a larger clutch for a casual night out. It will add sophistication to a dull outfit.

March

| | | | |
|---|---|---|---|
| Plan summer holidays | | | Check your skiing kit and replace what's worn or missing |
| 1 | 2 | 3 | 4 |
| 9 | 10 | 11 | 12 |
| | Book a facial | | |
| 17 | 18 | 19 | 20 |
| 25 | 26 | 27 | 28 |

MARCH

58

| | | | Write a list of everything you love about your life |
|---|---|---|---|
| 5 | 6 | 7 | 8 |
| | | Have your children's feet measured | |
| 13 | 14 | 15 | 16 |
| Turn over your mattress | | | |
| 21 | 22 | 23 | 24 |
| | | | |
| 29 | 30 | 31 | |

'If you're at a dinner party and want to check a disputed fact, text your question to 63336 for the correct answer.'

# HOW TO ENJOY YOUR OWN

# PARTY

## Saving time in the kitchen...

### ✳ Pressed for time? Buy online

Ok, recipes picked, now it's time to buy the ingredients. We suggest you do this online from the comfort of your own desk. Our absolute favourite food website is www.ocado.co.uk. This is the Waitrose internet and home delivery service that is backed up by www.waitrosedelivery.co.uk in areas a little more off the beaten track. And most importantly, you can save lists of your most regular items and, on a return visit, one click and it's winging its way to you.

### ✳ Devise the menu

It's important to devise the menu BEFORE you go shopping. There are some great cookbooks specialising in recipes that can be prepared in advance. Cook Now, Eat Later by Mary Berry is one we use a lot.

###  THINKING AHEAD

of time is the key. Do as much as possible the night before and morning of and you will free yourself up to have a blast and be the perfect hostess.

# SHOPPING LIST:

Butcher

Flowers

Fruit and veg

Drinks

Household etc

'I'm always pressed for time so
I don't go near the supermarket.
I can find everything I need at the
local shops and online at
ocado.com'

# MENU:

Starter

Main course

Pudding

'I've served this easy
peasy menu many times.
It always works a treat.'

# EASY PEASY
# MENU

### Shell-on prawns with mayonnaise

Buy a double handful per person
of cooked prawns with their shells on.
Put them in a large decorative bowl
for friends to pick from.
To a bowl of Hellman's mayonnaise,
add one egg yolk, lots of black pepper
and the juice of one lemon. It will
look and taste homemade.

### Chicken à la cheat

This recipe can be prepared in advance
and left in the fridge all day.
Allow one well-seasoned chicken breast
per person. Place in an ovenproof dish.
Pour over good quality bottled tomato or
arrabiata sauce. Put a slice of mozzarella
onto each breast and top with a basil
leaf. Shove in a medium-hot oven for
30-40 minutes until the cheese is golden
and bubbly like a pizza. Serve with a
green salad or pre-topped and tailed
French beans and new potatoes.

### Fooled you raspberry pud

Vanilla ice cream
Amaretti biscuits
Raspberries
Sprinkle crushed Amaretti biscuits over
scoops of ice cream and add a few
raspberries for colour.
Serve Maltesers with herb teas and
coffee at the end of the meal.

The most important element in a successful dinner, apart from food, wine and guests, is that you look comfortably

rather than fashionably uptight and overdressed. This will make you feel relaxed and put your guests at ease.

# DO

**Wear a long flowing skirt with bare feet or flat slippers.**

If you have long legs you can have bare feet peeping from your trousers.

**Match your scented candles to your fragrance so that you appear to be in all places at once, without being too overpowering.**

Candlelight everywhere covers up old carpet stains, where the kids have been on a rampage and the dog has dried itself after a muddy walk.

**Don't save money on cheap fragrance-scented candles that are not dissimilar to an air-freshener.**

Turn off all overhead lights. Your girlfriends will thank you for the flattering and intimate atmosphere it will create.

**Cut flowers short for the table, they look more luxurious and also allow for unencumbered conversations.**

# DON'T

Wear a jacket inside your own home, you will look like you are about to leave.

Wear too much make-up.

Have your hair professionally put up.

Wear black if it's not your colour. It will only make you look tired and friends will notice.

Wear boots – fine for a restaurant or the daytime, but too heavy for your own home.

# EFFORTLESSLY BE A GRACIOUS HOSTESS

# WHO
## TO INVITE?

People most enjoy a dinner of either
very old friends they haven't seen for ages or
meeting new people among old friends. Always
remember this when deciding
how to seat everyone.

A squashed table is sometimes more fun
than a formal one. If your table takes 6 fill it with
8, if 8 fill it with 10. It will create an extra level of
intimacy, and spark conversation more easily.

Remember when inviting single people that
they will feel less stressed if they already know
someone else at the dinner. And this gives
you more time to flit around the room
introducing people.

If you cannot remember someone's name,
ask the two people you're introducing: 'Have you
both met?', and they should end up introducing
themselves as you gracefully move onto the next
guest and away from the tricky situation.

# HOW TO DO A
# PARTY PLACEMENT

## The matchmaking dinner

When matchmaking two people, make sure the woman is seated between her potential match and someone who will bring out the best in her. So the man on the other side is aware of how funny/intelligent/sexy she is. Ditto with the man.

## Loud friends

If you have 2 or 3 loud friends never put them in a block but scatter them around the table with the more timid of your guests.

## Make sure

that you seat known kitchen-helping friends on the outside so they have easier access to the dishwasher.

## Going well

If the dinner is going really well don't break it up by moving to the sitting room for coffee, but if on the other hand it's lulling a move of location will get people chatting again.

## Lulls in conversation

if there are a few lulls in conversation, after the main course get the men to move two places to their right and give the dinner a new lease of life.

# ORGANISING THE TABLE

Write everyone's names on little strips of paper and arrange
them around an eggcup, to represent a round table, or a
matchbox, to represent an oblong table. This will allow you
to swap and reshuffle your guests until you feel you
have the balance exactly right, with no danger of
accidentally leaving someone out.

# PARTY ON A SHOESTRING

Remember friends don't want to be impressed and dazzled – they just want to see you and have fun. A bit of planning will make a wonderful party for not so many £££s and allow you to spend maximum time with your guests.

## Make up

some big jugs of mixed juice. Add a few berries, mint leaves and orange slices so that it looks like a gorgeous cocktail. Given the choice, it's surprising how many people choose the non-alcoholic option (they can always add their own vodka).

## A BIG BUNCH

of mixed flowers (whatever is going cheap on the market) can be cut short and placed singly in glasses and cups all around your home.

## Nobody minds

bringing a bottle but it helps if you let guests know what to bring. Work out a menu of drinks and ask your friends to stick to it. That way you don't end up with a sickening assortment of gin, beer, advocaat, sparkling wine and Bacardi Breezers.

## Cocktails

made from one base spirit (vodka, gin or rum) will work out less expensive than good wine – and the hangovers will be less profound too.

## Turn down the main lights

and make your home into an enchanted grotto with fairy lights and tea-light candles.

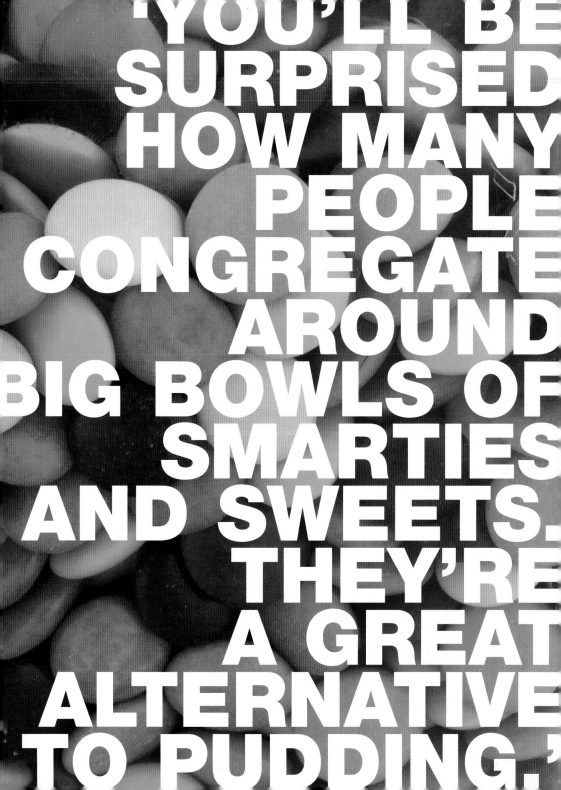

'YOU'LL BE SURPRISED HOW MANY PEOPLE CONGREGATE AROUND BIG BOWLS OF SMARTIES AND SWEETS. THEY'RE A GREAT ALTERNATIVE TO PUDDING.'

# DRESSES THE RULES

## Big tits

A scooped neckline gives the most flattering shape. The stripe across the boob area halves the perceived size of the breast.

A wrap lifts and separates chest area. The gather of the wrap draws the eye towards the waist.

## No tits

A plunging neckline can only be carried off by the flat-chested.

Black halter-necks show off great shoulders and hide what's not there. A low-cut back allows lots of sexy flesh to show.

## Big arms

The gathered and flared sleeve camouflages the actual arm size.

The contrast in the size of the batwing sleeve makes the lower arm appear smaller.

# Big tum

Vertical gathers around the tummy area make flab seem indistinguishable from the folds of fabric.

Diagonal stripes detract from the tummy flab and draw the eye to the cleavage.

# Thick calves

The hem ends at the upper ankle hiding the thick calf.

The hem of the dress ends at the narrowest part of the leg (just under the knee) and detracts from thick calves.

# Broad shoulders

Strapless dresses show off broad shoulders to best advantage.

A shirt dress draws the eye to the buttons down the middle and away from the breadth of the shoulder.

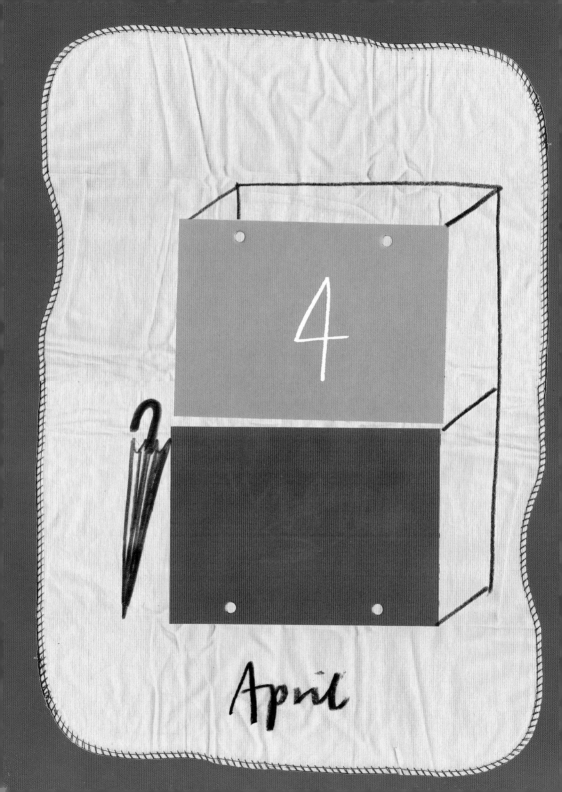

4

April

| | | | |
|---|---|---|---|
| Watch out! It's April Fool's Day<br><br>1 | Plant your window boxes<br><br>2 | 3 | 4 |
| 9 | 10 | 11 | 12 |
| 17 | Think about having a new style and colour for your hair<br><br>18 | 19 | 20 |
| 25 | 26 | 27 | 28 |

| | | | |
|---|---|---|---|
| 5 | 6 | 7 | 8 |
| | | Spring cleaning – check for signs of moths | |
| 13 | 14 | 15 | 16 |
| Book a dental check-up for the children | | | |
| 21 | 22 | 23 | 24 |
| | | | |
| 29 | 30 | | |

'If you are staying in a hotel on business, remember to take clothes to relax in after a long day.'

# HOW TO PACK

With meticulous planning we manage to pack everything we need into a holdall. It hasn't always been the case. Susannah used to turn up at the airport with only the clothes on her back, while Trinny would arrive for a weekend away lugging the contents of her house in a steamer trunk.

Remember that even if you're going somewhere hot it will be chilly on the plane. Always bring a light sweater, cardigan or pashmina. Think about how much you will be walking and on how many occasions you will want to look smart. Pack at least two pairs of shoes. One for comfort and one for glamour. Natural fibres like cotton, silk and wool can endure more wearings than synthetics without becoming too smelly.

TW

Orange dress

Coat

Yellow dress

Jumper

Chiffon top

Jeans

Trousers

Jacket

Necklace

Black belt

Sunglasses

Evening purse

Alice band

Earrings

Ring

Yellow belt

Shoulder bag

Sandals

Platform shoes

Trainers

**Always slip a small evening purse into your holdall. It will finish a smart or evening outfit so much better than your big shoulder bag.** By the third day your hair will be greasy. Bring a stylish headband to smarten it up. **Bold accessories**

Travelling there.

Friday night.

Saturday sightseeing.

**change the tone of an outfit, so you can wear it twice.** If you're a compulsive shopper, jewellery is the thing to buy on a weekend break. It won't add much to your luggage, isn't too heavy, and it will bring back fond memories every time you wear it.

Saturday
dinner.

Sunday
lunch.

Travelling
home.

# Where to go for a weekend

With thanks to Bernadette Carey of Parador Business travel: www.paradortravel.com  Flight times are from London.

| City | Flight time | Where to stay | A great book to read | What to look out for |
|---|---|---|---|---|
| **Amsterdam** | 1.10 | www.sevenbridgeshotel.nl £–££ Ambassade Hotel www.ambassade-hotel.nl ££ Blakes www.dylanamsterdam.com £££ | *Amsterdam* by Ian McEwan *The Diary of Anne Frank* | The Van Gogh museum The Floating Flower market Great duty free shopping at Schipol airport |
| **Barcelona** | 2.05 | Hosteria Grau www.hostalgrau.com £ Hotel Arts www.ritzcarlton.com/hotels/barcelona £££ | *Shadow of the Wind* by Carlos Ruiz Zafon | All the Gaudi buildings and his Parc Guell. The new port development has the best nightlife. Buy: fans, almonds, jamon, and clothes from Zara (they're 30% cheaper than in the UK) |
| **Berlin** | 1.45 | www.alexander-plaza.com £ The Radisson SAS has the world's largest aquarium in the lobby www.berlin.radissonsas.com ££ Hotel Adlon www.hotel-adlon.de £££ | *The Spy Who Came in from the Cold* by John le Carré. *The Dark Room* by Rachel Seiffert *Defying Hitler* by Sebastian Haffner | The Holocaust Memorial designed by Peter Eisenman is a must. The Reichstag Frank Gehry's DG Bank Buy: traditional toys or a Mercedes-Benz |
| **Biarritz** | 1.50 | Nere-Chocoa www.nerechocoa.com £ Hotel du Palais www.hotel-du-palais.com £££ | *Ramuntcho* by Pierre Loti | The beach Buy: divine chocolate |
| **Budapest** | 2.30 | Mercure Budapest Duna www.mercure.com £ Four Seasons Gresham Palace www.fourseasons.com/budapest £££ | *Embers* by Sandor Marai | The Hapsburg Palace and the old city. The spa at the Gellert Hotel Buy: needlepoint and Hungarian wines |
| **Copenhagen** | 1.50 | Hotel Fox www.hotelfox.dk 21 young designers worked on the hotel to create an ecclectic, mad mix of individual rooms £–££ | *The Little Mermaid* by Hans Christian Andersen *Miss Smilla's Feeling for Snow* by Peter Hoek | The Tivoli Gardens The Little Mermaid Rosenborg Castle Buy: china, glassware and needlepoint |

| City | Flight time | Where to stay | A great book to read | What to look out for |
|------|-------------|---------------|----------------------|----------------------|
| **Dublin** | 1.20 | Grafton House www.graftonguesthouse.com £ Merrion Hotel www.merrionhotel.com £££ | *Quentins* by Maeve Binchy | Patrick's restaurant Trinity College Go browsing at Brown Thomas Buy: a souvenir teapot from Bewley's |
| **Florence** | 2.00 | Residenze Johanna & Johlea www.johanna.it £ Hotel Il Guelfo Bianco www.ilguelfobianco.it ££ Villa San Michele www.villasanmichele.com £££ | *A Room with a View* by E. M. Forster | Michelangelo's David The Uffizi Gallery The Pitti Palace Harold Actons' villa overlooking Florence Designer clothes from outlet stores Buy: Santa Maria Novella pot-pourri. You have to buy a new handbag! |
| **Istanbul** | 3.45 | Hotel Empress Zoe www.emzoe.com £ Four Seasons www.fourseasons.com/istanbul £££ | *The Sultan's Seal* by Jenny White | The medina Hagia Sofia The harem at the royal palace is a great insight into royal life Take a boat trip on Bosphorus Buy: carpets, jewellery and fake designer bags |
| **Lisbon** | 2.50 | Novotel Lisboa www.novotel.com £ Lapa Palace – Expensive – www.lapapalace.com £££ | *A Small Death in Lisbon* by Robert Wilson | The Monastery of Jeronimos The Gulbenkian Museum Buy: tiles |
| **Madrid** | 2.25 | Tryp Alondras www.solmelia.com £ Hotel Ritz www.ritzmadrid.com £££ | *Captain Alatriste* by Arturo Perez-Reverte | Goyas in the Prado The Royal Palace The churros and hot chocolate are a sweet toother's dream |
| **Marrakech** | 3.30 | Dar Mouassine www.darmouassine.com £-££ Kasbah Tamadot www.virginlimitededition.co.uk ££ Aman Jena www.amanpuri.com/jena £££ | *Stolen Lives: Twenty Years in a Desert Jail* by Malika Oufkir with Michele Fitoussi *Hideous Kinky* by Esther Freud | The Medina The Royal Palace Djemaa El Fna The main square at night comes alive with snake charmers etc. Don't eat from the stalls unless you have a strong constitution Buy: slippers, lanterns and pottery |
| **Monte Carlo** | 1.55 to Nice | Columbus www.columbushotels.com £ Hotel Hermitage www.montecarloresort.com £££ | *Casino Royale* by Ian Fleming | The Casino The Aquarium The beach club. Go to San Remo round the corner and buy handbags and belts at the market |

| City | Flight time | Where to stay | A great book to read | What to look out for |
|---|---|---|---|---|
| **Naples** | 2.45 | Napolit'Amo www.napolitamo.it £ Grand Hotel Vesuvio www.vesuvio.it £££ | *Pompeii* by Robert Harris | The old city walls Don't miss Capri and Pompeii when you are there Buy: men's ties made to measure and as much Napoli ice cream as you can eat |
| **New York** | 7.25 | Hotel QT www.hotelqt.com £-££ Hotel on Rivington www.hotelonrivington.com £££ Soho House www.sohohouseny.com £££ 4 Seasons www.fourseasons.com £££ Mercer www.mercerhotel.com £££ | *The Kinky Friedman Crime Club* by Kinky Friedman *Bonfire of the Vanities* by Tom Wolfe *Sex and the City* by Candace Bushnall | The Empire State Building The Statue of Liberty Central Park The Metropolitan Museum The Oyster Bar at Grand Central Station The Frick Museum Shopping in Soho Buy: sportswear from Abercrombie & Fitch and watches from around 47th Street *See our shopping guide* |
| **Nice and the French Riviera** | 1.55 to Nice | Hotel Windsor Nice www.hotelwindsornice.com ££ Hotel Belles-Rives at Juan les Pins www.bellesrives.com £££ Hotel du Cap Eden Roc at Cap d'Antibes (credit cards are not accepted) www.edenroc-hotel.fr £££ | *Tender is the Night* by F. Scott Fitzgerald | Albert 1st gardens Old town streets The antique market The Chagall Museum The Museum of Modern Art has a garden designed by Yves Klein on the roof. The children's zoo at Cap Ferrat Yacht watching at St Tropez Buy: lavender soaps. Eat at La Petite Maison for the best bouillabaisse: +33 4 93 92 59 59 and Tetou for truffles: +33 4 93 63 71 16 |
| **Paris** | 2.50 by Eurostar | Any hotel in the Best Western chain. www.bestwestern.world executive.com £-££ Park Hyatt, Vendome www.paris.park.hyatt.com ££ Hotel Costes www.hotelcostes.com £££ The Ritz www.ritzparis.com £££ | *The Pursuit of Love* by Nancy Mitford *Perfume* by Patrick Suskind | Sacre Coeur The Latin Quarter The Rodin Museum The Eiffel Tower The Flea Market at Clignancourt *See our shopping guide* |
| **Prague** | 1.55 | Hotel U Brany www.ubrany.cz ££ Four Seasons www.fourseasons.com/ prague £££ | *The Unbearable Lightness of Being* by Milan Kundera | The Old Town square Wenceslas Square The C18th Estates Theatre where Mozart conducted the world premiere of his Don Giovanni in 1787 Charles Bridge Buy: crystal glasses and vases, antiques |

| City | Flight time) | Where to stay | A great book to read | What to look out for |
|---|---|---|---|---|
| **Reykjavik** | 3.00 | Radisson SAS 1919<br>www.radissonsas.com<br>££ | *The Killer's Guide to Iceland* by Zane Radcliffe | The Pearl Observatory<br>The Blue Lagoon<br>Buy: Aquavit |
| **Rome** | 2.30 | Hotel del Sole<br>www.hotelsolealpantheon.com<br>££<br>Hotel de Russie<br>http://www.hotelderussie.it<br>£££ | *Roman Holiday* by Belle Reilly | There are so many unmissable treasures. Take a horse and buggy ride to see them all. If you need a walk, stroll through the magnificent Borghesi Gardens<br>Buy: shoes and leather goods. |
| **Seville** | 2.40 | Casas de los Mercaderes<br>www.intergrouphoteles.com<br>£<br>Hotel Alfonso XII<br>www.hotel-alfonsoxiii.com<br>£££ | *The Blind Man of Seville* by Robert Wilson | Giralda Tower<br>Triana district<br>Alcazar Palace<br>Buy: shawls and fans |
| **St Petersburg** | 3.15 | Hotel Astoria<br>www.astoria.spb.ru<br>£££ | *Nicholas and Alexandra* by Robert K. Massie | Peter and Paul Fortress<br>The Hermitage Museum<br>Buy: fur hats, china, caviar, wooden and papier-mâché toys |
| **Stockholm** | 2.10 | Pensionat Oden<br>www.pensionat.nu<br>£<br>Grand Hotel<br>www.grandhotel.se<br>£££ | *Faceless Killers* by Henning Mankell | Take a ferry to the islands<br>Royal Palace<br>City Hall<br>The Design Museum<br>Buy: cutlery, anything by Georg Jensen |
| **Venice** | 2.20 | Hotel Flora www.hotelflora.it<br>£<br>Palazzo San'Angelo<br>www.santangelo.hotelinvenice.com<br>££<br>Cipriani www.hotelcipriani.com<br>£££ | *Through a Glass Darkly* by Donna Leon<br>*Death in Venice* by Thomas Mann<br>*Miss Garnet's Angel* by Sally Vickers | St Mark's Square<br>Rialto Bridge<br>Bridge of Sighs<br>Palazzo Ducale<br>Buy: Murano glass (but make sure that it's not made in China!) and writing paper.<br>*See our shopping guide* |
| **Vienna** | 2.25 | Pension Neuer Markt<br>www.hotelpension.at<br>£<br>Hotel Kaiserin Elisabeth<br>www.kaiserinelisabeth.at<br>££<br>Hotel Imperial<br>www.starwoodhotels.com<br>£££ | *The Third Man* by Graham Greene.<br>*Vienna* by Eva Menasse | Take a buggy ride.<br>See the Spanish Riding school, the State Opera House and St Stephan's Cathedral<br>Buy: sacher torte, hand-knitted socks and sweaters. |

# FAB IDEAS
## FOR A FEW DAYS AWAY

## Release your spirit

**Want to totally transform your life in a few days? There are many amazing self-improvement workshops available. These are the ones that have worked for us and for many of our friends.**

The Hoffman Process. An eight-day residential programme for overcoming counter-productive belief systems and negative, self-defeating behaviours. www.hoffmaninstitute.org

LifeWorks offers five-day non-residential workshops focusing on the family, life transformation and developing spirituality. www.lifeworkscommunity.com

World-renowned celebrity clinic Cottonwood de Tuscon in Arizona runs a programme of one-week Inner Path Retreats, focusing on relationships, co-dependency, grief and loss, past trauma or women's issues. www.innerpathretreats.com. One- and two-day non-residential workshops in London can be arranged through their website. www.cottonwood.ltd.uk

Outlook Training is a three-day non-residential course focusing on unblocking negative behaviour and setting new goals. www.outlooktraining.org

The Alexander Technique is a transformational approach to posture and body awareness. For UK residential courses visit: www.stat.org.uk

Get mind and body into harmony with a yoga holiday in England or abroad: www.simonlow.com or www.yogaonashoestring.com

Chrysalis is a residential holistic centre in West Wicklow, Ireland. Offering courses throughout the year in physical and spiritual development. www.chrysalis.ie

# Regenerate

In the bad old days, consumption sufferers were dispatched to Europe's spa towns, and more recently 'Health Farms' were renowned for boot-camp regimes coupled with starvation diets. Thankfully, the world has changed. Now we look forward to languorous breaks designed to totally recharge our batteries at hot springs and baths.

Popes and Princes have bathed in the curative waters at Bagno Vignoni in southern Tuscany. This tiny hamlet offers a range of breaks. Try the 5-star Adler Thermae www.adler-thermae.com; mid-priced Hotel Posta Marcucci www.hotelpostamarcucci.it; less expensive Albergo Le Terme www.albergoleterme.it; or a gorgeous bed and breakfast La Locanda del Loggiato www.loggiato.it

Iceland's Blue Lagoon is world-famed for its astonishingly blue geothermally heated waters, believed to be particularly helpful for psoriasis and skin conditions. www.bluelagoon.is. A less crowded alternative is the beautiful Myvatn Baths near Iceland's northern city of Akureyri www.jardbodin.is

You've seen the photos of fat blokes playing chess while enjoying the waters of Budapest's Széchenyi Spa. It is actually a huge complex of swimming and bathing pools saunas and steam rooms decorated with mosaics and fountains. Believed to be helpful in treating arthritis and degenerative disorders of joints and the spine. A guide to Hungary's famous spas can be found at www.spa.hu

Britain has been without a natural hot water spa for decades. Crazy, isn't it, when one has existed at Bath since Roman times? Long overdue and wildly over budget, the new Bath Spa was due to open at the time this book went to press – but didn't. We still want you to have the information and really look forward to having a hot water spa in our own country. Keep up with developments at www.thermaebathspa.com

A Turkish hammam is not a swirling steam room but rather a heated marble slab where you recline, get swatted and then soaped down by a burly attendant. Built in 1584, Cemberlitas is one of Istanbul's finest www.cemberlitashamami.com.tr. Or check out the newer (18th century!) Cagaloglu hammam www.cagagloghuhamami.com.tr

The West Coast of Ireland is famed for its health-giving seaweed baths. A hot bath steeped in seaweed leaves the skin enriched and feeling about 15 years younger. Kilcullen's Seaweed Baths, Enniscrone, Co. Sligo. Tel: +353 96 36 238; Celtic Seaweed Baths, Strandhill, Co. Sligo. Tel: +353 71 916 8686

Snuggling up is the natural thing to do at the end of a wild and windswept walk. Book a winter walking holiday in the Peak District or along the Cornish cliffs. Rent a cosy cottage with an open fireplace for evening cuddles.

Get scared silly and then rush into your partner's protective arms. Haunted house holidays are available at www.hauntedhotelguide.com

Find new shared passions in your 60s, 70s and 80s. Celebrity chef Rick Stein runs residential fish cookery courses at his Padstow HQ. www.rickstein.com

Love the country, learn the language. Residential language courses abroad are available through www.cactuslanguage.com

Toscana Photographic Workshop organises residential courses run by master photographers in the Tuscan countryside. www.tpw.it

Learn to do what your partner loves, be it playing golf, pot-holing, rally driving or even trainspotting. Organise a holiday where you learn and he gets to show off and strut his stuff.

A fabulous bed and a great view are all that we require of a romantic hotel. For the most sumptuous seaside snuggles, try Hotel Tresanton at St Mawes, Cornwall: www.tresanton.com

Cliveden House at Taplow, Berkshire, has the grandest rooms at top prices: www.clivedenhouse.co.uk

The Hotel du Vin chain all have lovely comfy beds. As a bonus, their excellent wine tastings will get you into relaxed mood: www.hotelduvin.com

A railway sleeper compartment forces you both to get really close, with the atmosphere of being in an old-time movie. Bunk up on the train overnight and finish the journey feasting your eyes on some of the most beautiful scenery in Britain. London to Fort William by train: www.nationalrail.co.uk

For a more leisurely descent into cabin fever, try boating the length of Ireland's Shannon River. www.shannon-river.com or www.cruise-ireland.com

If all else fails go to Venice.

**Wherever you're headed, there are a few essential steps to make sure things go smoothly.**

- Leave your laptop and Blackberry behind.
- Don't tell too many people where you're going.
- Change your voicemail message to say that you're away and please only leave a message if it is urgent. This prevents irritating trivial matters bugging you.
- Remember to take your iPod with all your special music (don't forget the leads and speakers).
- Bring a box of tealight candles to create a romantic atmosphere in your hotel room.
- If you haven't had sex for a while, chill out. It may not happen on the first evening. Relax into a renewed intimacy first and see what happens from there.

REKINDLE

There are
endless brochures and
websites specialising in
romantic getaways for
couples and honeymooners,
but let's face it, in the first
flush of love a bus shelter
would seem like Shangri-
La. After a few years of
daily togetherness,
romance sometimes
needs a kick
start.

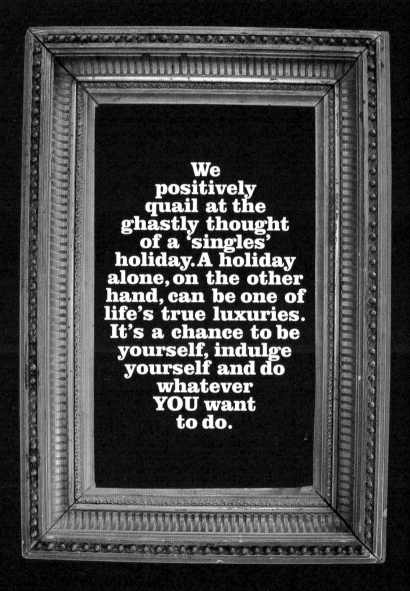

We
positively
quail at the
ghastly thought
of a 'singles'
holiday. A holiday
alone, on the other
hand, can be one of
life's true luxuries.
It's a chance to be
yourself, indulge
yourself and do
whatever
YOU want
to do.

# GOING IT
# ALONE

## Holiday in your own town

You know that gorgeous hotel that you gaze longingly at from the bus window as you pass by every drizzly evening? Just book in there for a long weekend. Don't tell anyone where you're going. Then go mad doing all the cheesy, touristy things that you normally look down your nose at. Take a tour bus, visit the sights, go to a show, eat alone in the swankiest restaurant (demand their best table) and finally flop back to your hotel to watch movies and eat room-service ice cream in bed.

## Literary breaks

Great writers can invoke the very spirit of a particular place. Have you ever read a book that makes you think that you can almost smell and feel the surroundings? Grab the book and go there. Be an amateur detective and ferret out all the locations mentioned.
Some ideas: The Grimm Brothers' fairy tales were collected mainly from the areas around Hanover and Hessen in Germany.
Ian Rankin's Inspector Rebus mysteries positively drip with the air of Edinburgh.
London, The Biography by Peter Ackroyd is the ultimate book to discover London. See our Destination Information for lots more ideas.

## Reading retreat

Oh, the luxury of being able to spend a week alone catching up with all the books you meant to read.
Some ideas: rent a folly from the Landmark Trust (www.landmarktrust.org.uk) and enjoy windswept walks between chapters.
Glenstal Abbey is a Benedictine monastery set in a 500-acre estate in County Limerick, Ireland. Simple accommodation is offered in the guesthouse. www.glenstal.com

## Gallery tours

Only when travelling alone can we take time to truly immerse ourselves in Europe's spectacular art galleries and museums free of demands for wee-wees, popcorn and side trips to car showrooms. Explore London's British Museum and the Victoria and Albert Museum (only seven miles of corridors); Le Louvre in Paris; Florence's Uffizi Gallery; the Museo del Prado in Madrid; or the magnificent Hermitage Museum in St Petersburg. Avoid feeling like one of the herd – push out the boat and hire a personal guide for the day.

## Go to Florence

and shop yourself stupid in the outlet stores:
The Mall: Armani, Fendi, Gucci, Bottega Veneta and more: www.outlet-firenze.com
Roberto Cavalli: www.robertocavallioutlet.it
Space: Prada, Miu-Miu, Helmut Lang,
Tel: +39 055 978 9481
Dolce & Gabana: Tel: +39 055 833 111
Fendi: Tel: +39 055 834 981
Gucci: Tel: +39 055 865 7775
For the utmost in luxury, hire a personal driver and fashion guide at www.exclusivetuscany.com

## How to get rid of the kids

You know you're dumping your kids, but they think you're treating them to a fabulous adventure at summer camp.

For lots of ideas try: www.pgl.co.uk; www.summerfun4kids.co.uk; www.campbeaumont.co.uk or www.kidsklub.co.uk. The British Activity Holiday Association has a directory at www.baha.org.uk

Night Nannies will arrive at 9 p.m and stay until 7 a.m. Have a night out on the tiles or just an uninterrupted sleep in your own bed. www.night-nannies.com

# SKIRTS THE RULES

## Big bum

A structured pencil skirt hugs the bum and holds it all in place.

The fishtails balance out the bum size.

Fluted chiffon hem softens the bum and leads the eye downwards.

## No hips

The inverted pleats give a more curvy shape to the body.

The detail on the hip gives an illusion of an hourglass shape.

A gathered waistband adds volume and shape to the hips.

# Big tummy

A wrap skirt allows the wearer to adjust the fit over the tummy and pull it in until It looks exactly right.

Big sash detail conceals larger tummy.

The twisted knot at the waistband and the soft pleating of the skirt hide the tummy bulge underneath

# Saddlebags

The length of the skirt takes the eye away from the size of the hips.

A-line is the best cut for skimming over saddlebags.

Uneven hem detail draws the eye away from the saddlebags.

| | | | |
|---|---|---|---|
| Pack away your winter woollies, boots and shoes<br><br>1 | 2 | 3 | 4 |
| 9 | 10 | 11 | 12 |
| 17 | Clean out bathroom cupboards and throw out old cosmetics<br><br>18 | 19 | If you're nervous about wearing a bikini, cut out cappuccino and croissants now<br><br>20 |
| 25 | 26 | 27 | 28 |

| 5 | 6 | 7 | 8 |
|---|---|---|---|
| | | Book a manicure and pedicure | |
| 13 | 14 | 15 | 16 |
| | | | |
| 21 | 22 | 23 | 24 |
| | | Dry clean winter coats and jackets and put them away | |
| 29 | 30 | 31 | |

'If you discover your best shoes of all time, go back to the shop a week later and buy a second pair before they sell out. You will never regret it.'

## Spiritual solutions

After sun damage and smoking, the biggest factors that age us are anger and stress. Taken together on a daily basis they add a lot of misery and tiredness to a face. Here are some suggestions to counter anger and stress. Small changes on the inside can trigger big changes on the outside.

# THE ART OF NOT LOOKING YOUR AGE

**Each morning** ask your higher power for love and protection.

**Every evening** thank your higher power for all the experiences, challenges and benefits of your day.

### Resentments

Accepting rather than resenting the past allows us to approach today with love rather than with anger. The past is over, and cannot be changed. The future does not yet exist. The only thing I can change is right now.

### Breathe deeply

If feeling panicked or breathless, cross your hands over the centre of your chest, between your breasts (this is the heart chakra). Breathe slowly and regularly in and out through your nose until you feel settled.

Remember the journey is as important as the destination. Do your part of whatever is required, then let go of the result.

**Look for the positive** aspect in every situation. It may not be obvious but it is there.

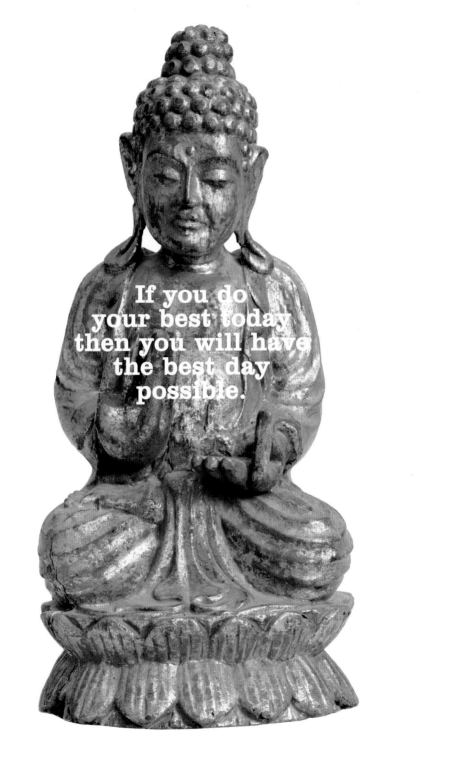

If you do
your best today
then you will have
the best day
possible.

### A long bath

How often do you have those 'Eureka!' moments? A long bath with no radio or telephone allows the brain to unwind as well as the body. Giving freedom to the mind allows it to be creative.

Try going without newspapers and the television for a week. They fill our brains with a relentless diet of drama and chaos. (Don't fret, if World War Three breaks out you can be sure someone will tell you.) Listen to music and read books. Observe how calm and free-thinking you become after a few days.

# WAYS TO MEDITATE

Instead of pounding away in front of an aerobics video, go for a long walk in your MBTs. Rhythmic walking is a great form of meditation.

### Light a candle

Focus on the candle flame and notice all the colours and the way it moves. This will help you empty your mind. Thoughts will intrude, just let them float away. Keep bringing your attention back to the flame. Start with a few minutes and build it up. You don't have to do this every night, but we both find that the more we do it the easier it gets.

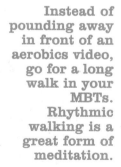

Please
help me to love
and forgive myself.
Help me to forgive everyone
who has hurt me and let them
go in peace. Ask for forgiveness
from everyone that I have hurt
consciously or unconsciously.
Help me to accept myself as
I am. I am a part of your
world. I feel your
light within me.
I am free.

# BEAUTY TIPS

**Go to bed early** Sleeping is not a waste of precious time. It is your body's most valuable time. Make sure that your bed is as calm, comfortable and inviting as possible.

**Camomile tea** A cup of camomile tea at bedtime helps to bring forth sweet dreams.

**Pillow spray** Use a heavenly pillow spray to create a sense of relaxation and well being.

**Fish oils** are brain food. Eat three portions of oily fish a week: sardines, salmon, mackerel, anchovies, trout and herrings all count.

**Massage** Release your subconscious with a deep, relaxing head massage. Our experience is that dreams become more vivid in the following nights. Indulge yourself with a massage, reflexology or a similar therapy that will make you feel pampered and wonderful. Take a day off and give yourself a home facial, manicure and pedicure.

**Drink lots of water** Two litres a day is recommended to flush out toxins and keep the skin hydrated and looking good.

**Sing** It expands the lungs and makes you feel great. Let the neighbours think what they want to.

**Detox once a year** Every major world religion includes a period of fasting, a recognition that it is necessary to rest our digestive systems periodically. The Western diet, rich in fats, meat, refined sugar and wheat, can leave us feeling tired and sluggish. There are plenty of seven-day detox diets around, ranging from complete fasting to juice or raw energy diets. Browse the internet or check out your local bookstore to find one that suits you. Our favourite detox gurus are Dr Gillian McKeith and Leslie Kenton.

# EAT YOUR WAY TO
# GORGEOUSNESS

Getting married next week, but still recovering from your hen night? Dr Nicholas Perricone recommends going on a face-saving diet for two or three days before a big event. We've adapted it from his book, The Wrinkle Cure:

## Breakfast

Fresh fruit salad, including lots of berries.
Slow-cooked porridge made with water. Add some slices of apple and a shake of cinnamon when it is nearly cooked.
Herbal tea.

## Lunch

A slice of grilled, organic salmon.
Salad of Cos lettuce leaves dressed with olive oil and lemon juice.
Green tea.

## Dinner

Steamed mixed vegetables including: broccoli, mixed peppers, green beans and cauliflower.
Slices of cantaloupe or honeydew melon.
Camomile tea.

> '**Nature gives you the face you have at 20; it is up to you to merit the face you have at 50.**'
>
> Coco Chanel

That was in 1956. Her famous proclamation, since repeated by generations of women, has at last been made obsolete by amazing new technologies. We both believe that it is now possible to age gracefully without surgery.

Seeing our list on pages 104-5 you will be surprised to see how much can be achieved without fear of the knife. Our favourite non-surgical, anti-ageing expert, Dr Jean-Louis Sebagh, believes that 'Regular maintenance is the key to preventing invasive surgery. A combination of botox, fillers, radio frequency and a good skincare regime can ensure you attain a natural, healthy, glowing skin, always.'

The trick is to have small subtle procedures done gradually, thus avoiding dramatic changes in your visage. Don't wait until the ageing signs become drastic and irrevocable. Ideally, your friends will say, 'My goodness, don't you look well?' rather than 'Oh, I see she's been on a Botox binge.'

# NON-SURGICAL SOLUTIONS

## It is imperative that before you undertake any procedure you ask the following questions:

- How long have your practitioners been practising?
- What are their qualifications?
- Which professional bodies do they belong to?
- How long have they used the procedure you are about to undertake?
- Is the material to be used animal, human or bio-engineered?
- What clinical studies have been done?
- Is it licensed for cosmetic use?
- Are there any known side effects?
- Might I be allergic?
- Is the procedure reversible?
- How long does it last?
- Will there be any recovery time?
- How much are they going to charge?
- How many treatments are required to see a result?
- How often will top-ups be needed?
- Do they have testimonials from other patients?
- Can you talk to someone who has undertaken the procedure?

**Remember that personal recommendations are the most reliable.**

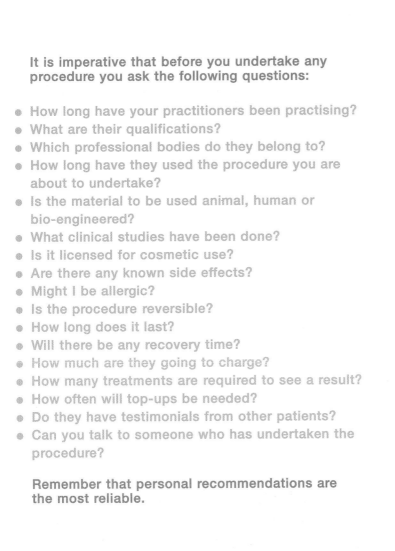

The costs (see over) are guidelines only based on London prices, but they should give you some idea of what you may be letting yourself in for. Total costs will vary, depending on how many sessions are needed, the profile of your practitioner and the plushness of their consulting rooms. Always ask for a firm price quote before committing yourself.

# Non-surgical procedures

With thanks to Dr Jean-Louis Sebagh and Dr Diana Mariton MD at The French Cosmetic Medical Company 020 7637 0548

| This is my problem | What's going on? | The solution | Be aware |
|---|---|---|---|
| **Lined forehead** | Frowning and raising the brow has broken down tissue over time, leaving furrows. | Botox. Botulinum toxin relaxes the muscles thereby making it physically impossible to crease the brow. Lasts three to six months. | You might bruise for four or five days. Too much Botox can cause an eyebrow to droop. Inexpert application can leave your face looking lopsided. Cost: from £300. |
| **Saggy jaw** | The skin is sagging through loss of underlying muscle and skin tone. | Polaris. A high radio frequency therapy that stimulates your own collagen production. It tightens and tautens the skin thereby redefining the jawline. Around six treatments are needed to see a long-term difference. Lasts 18-24 months or indefinitely if top-ups are taken every three months. | Approximately six treatments are needed to really see a long-term difference. Cost: from £300 per session. Initially six treatments over three months, then one top-up every three months. |
| **Saggy jaw** | The fat is travelling down your face. | Dream Sculpture  A sculpting technique pioneered by Dr Sebagh. Restalyne sub Q (hyaluronic acid) is injected at a deep level into the lower jaw. Lasts 15 months. | It hurts – quite a lot. Cost: from £800–1500. |
| **Dark circles** | The skin is thinning under your eyes. | Hyaluronic acid Injections to bolster the thin skin. High radio frequency treatments improve drainage thereby helping to reduce puffiness. Lasts nine months. | Dark circles are with you for life, but they can be alleviated with this treatment. Cost: from £300. |
| **Bags under eyes** | Fat hernia is coming through the muscle. | Good creams for temporary relief, such as Dr Sebagh's *For Your Eyes Only* cream should be applied daily. | Surgery is the only long-term solution. Effective creams are expensive (from £55). |
| **Lined lips** | Fine vertical lines, so-called 'smoking lines', are caused by lip movement over many years, mainly talking rather than smoking. | Botox around the lip line is the most effective treatment.The earlier you start the better for prevention. Lasts four to six months. | The doctor must use miniscule amounts so the muscles around the mouth are not weakened. Cost: from £250. |
| **Fine lines** | Collagen depletion. | Polaris high radio frequency + laser treatment, which works on all skin colours, tightens skin and boosts the collagen production thereby plumping out wrinkles. Lasts 18 months. | Needs to be undertaken by a qualified practitioner. High heating can burn the skin. Cost: from £300 per treatment. Six required. |
| **Ageing lips** | The area of skin above the lip is getting thinner causing the lips to lose their definition. | Hyaluronic acid to redefine the contour and fill the little lines running from the upper lip. High radio frequency treatments stimulate collagen production. Lasts 12 months. | Be careful not to overdo it and end up looking like you've been punched in the mouth. Cost: from £400. |

| This is my problem | What's going on? | The solution | Be aware |
|---|---|---|---|
| Thin lips | Something you are born with. | Hyaluronic acid is injected to plump lips proportionally to the shape of the face. Lasts 12 months. | Don't just do the top lip and end up looking like Donald Duck. Cost: from £400. |
| Crow's-feet | Smiling and facial expression has caused fine grooves in the skin. | Combination of Botox to stop further wrinkling movements, and Polaris to help re-plump the skin. Lasts four to six months. | Be careful not to do too much and freeze your face into an expressionless mask. Cost: from £400. |
| Recently lost weight and now your face is sagging | The youthful plumpness created by fat cells is lost and in some cases might never return. | Dr Sebagh has created a technique called *Dream Sculpture* (Deep Remodelling by Elevation And Mass Sculpture). Hyaluronic acid is injected at a deep level into the skin. It supports and prevents the sagging of the face and restores the volume. Lasts 15 months. | It is only available from Dr Sebagh. Cost: from £800–£1500. |
| Age spots | Sun damage causes over-production of melanin, creating dark spots. | Aurora Intensive Pulsed Light laser with high frequency. It lightens the pigmentation. Lasts forever if you stay out of the sun. | Cannot be done with a suntan, sunburn or on black skin. Best to have procedure done in winter. Cost: from £300 with two or three treatments required. |
| Rosacea | Broken capillaries beneath the skin cause a red bloom on the face. | Aurora and Polaris combined treatment cauterises the fine blood vessels. You might need a treatment once a year if new broken capillaries appear. | You must stay out of the sun. Cost: from £300 with two or three treatments required. |
| Enlarged pores | Hormonal changes cause sebaceous glands to become over active. | Polaris shrinks the sebaceous glands and closes the pores. Lasts indefinitely. | Wait until your hormones have settled down before undertaking treatment. Cost: from £300 with two to three treatments required. |
| Thread veins on the leg | Small veins have become enlarged and capillaries have broken. | Intensive Pulsed Light with high radio frequency treatment can improve appearance of smaller veins. No maintenance required, but new veins may develop. | Deep, large veins require surgery – Sclerotherapy. Cost: from £400 for both lower legs with three to four treatments required. |
| Acne | Sebaceous glands are stimulated by hormonal activity and then become infected. | Intensive Pulsed Light with high radio frequency treatment sterilises and reduces the sebaceous glands, Polaris helps to reduce scarring. Serious acne requires medical treatment by a qualified dermatologist. | You must stay out of the sun during treatment. Maintenance treatments as needed. Cost: from £300 with three treatments initially, then one every six to eight weeks until the hormones settle down. |
| Scarring | Elastin and collagen become depleted. | Polaris plumps up the skin and reduces ridging and puckering. Lasts two to three years. | It is not possible to re-pigment the whiteness caused by loss of elastin. Cost: from £300 with around six treatments required. |

# SURGICAL
# SOLUTIONS

Cosmetic surgery is almost commonplace these days. Many women consider it as an alternative to buying a new car or an annual holiday. This doesn't mean your decision should be taken lightly. Surgery will not make you younger, wittier or happier. It can, however, if undertaken with very careful consideration, give some women an enormous boost in self-confidence.

Top London plastic surgeon, Mr Peter Butler, says: 'Life takes its toll. Non-surgical and surgical approaches can be used to reverse the effects. For some women the only solution is surgery. I usually recommend a combination approach.'

Choosing your surgeon is important. It is said that many women spend more time choosing a pair of shoes than they do their plastic surgeon. But this is not a pair of shoes, it's your face and body, and they are not replaceable. See more than one surgeon to get a good overview of their opinions and recommendations before you make up your mind.

Research is key. Get recommendations from friends and acquaintances. Talk to your GP. Read articles on the internet. Read books and magazine articles about surgery in general and the procedure that you are considering in particular. We highly recommend the *Beauty Lowdown* series of books by Wendy Lewis: www.wlbeauty.com

It is important that you are as fit and healthy as possible before surgery. Ask your surgeon to guide you on preparing yourself physically and mentally.

It is imperative, as with non-surgical treatments, that before you undertake any procedure you find out the following about your surgeons:

- How long have they been practising and what are their qualifications?
- Are they members of the British Association of Aesthetic Plastic Surgeons (BAAPS) or another recognised professional body?
- How long and how often have they used the procedure that you are about to undertake?
- Who will perform the anaesthesia and what are the anaesthetist's qualifications?
- How long will the procedure take and what is the recovery time?
- How long will the results last?
- Can you see other patients' testimonials and 'before' and 'after' photographs?
- Can you talk to someone who has undertaken the procedure?
- What are the potential complications?
- What will the total cost be?
- What happens if something goes wrong?
- Have they had any legal action taken against them, or is any pending, as a result of any procedure they have performed?

The price guides below are based on surgical fees in London. There will be additional charges for the hospital stay and anaesthesia. Charges vary wildly, but cheaper does not always mean best. Be careful of cut-price deals. They may not include follow-ups, emergency surgery or revisional surgery if something goes wrong.

# Surgical procedures

With thanks to Mr Peter Butler, MD, FRCSI, FRCS(Eng), FRCS(Plast) at London Plastic Surgery Associates: www.lpsa.co.uk

| This is my problem | The Surgery | What should I know | What are the risks? |
|---|---|---|---|
| **BREASTS** | | | |
| **Too small or deflated after breastfeeding** | Breast enlargement (Breast augmentation) | A large choice of implants are available. Ask your surgeon about all the alternatives. Implants are placed either under breast tissue or under muscle. Choose a size appropriate to your body frame for a natural look. General anaesthetic required. Cost: from £2500. Lasts 10-20 years. | Implants can leak or rupture. Scar tissue can cause hardening of the breast. Implants can displace and look odd. Can cause a rippled skin effect. Choosing inappropriately large implants can leave you looking like a comic version of a page 3 girl. |
| **Sagging** | Breast-lift (Mastopexy) | Sagging is natural after childbirth or with age. Lift can be achieved with an implant if breast droop is mild. Otherwise excess skin may need to be removed and reshaped. General anaesthetic required. Cost: from £2600. Lasts 10 years. | Risk of scarring if a lot of reshaping is required. Risk of asymmetry. Possible loss of nipple sensation. May impair ability to breastfeed. |
| **Melons** | Breast reduction | Surgery to remove excess breast fat, gland and skin. General anaesthetic required. Cost: from £2600. Lasts indefinitely. | Risk of scars around nipple and under breast. See risks for Mastopexy, above. |
| **FACE** | | | |
| **Saggy face and jawline** | Face-lift (Rhytidectomy) | Many techniques are available from suture suspension with minimal scars to full face-lift. It is important to pick the right technique for your problem. Does not remove facial lines or replace lost volume – fillers are required for this. General anaesthetic required. Cost: from £4000. Lasts 10 years. | Scarring behind the ears (your hairdresser will be able to tell). Risk of damage to nerves that control the facial muscles. Overdoing it can cause your face to look like an expressionless death mask. |
| **Saggy neck** | Neck-lift (Platysmaplasty) | Usually performed in combination with a face-lift. There will be an additional small incision under the chin. General anaesthetic required.Cost: from £1500. Lasts 10 years. | A big turkey gobble is difficult to correct. Risks are the same as for a face-lift. |
| **Droopy eyes** | Eye- lift (Blepharoplasty) | Upper and lower lid surgery. Many techniques are practised depending on the problem. Crow's-feet and wrinkles are best treated with Botox and laser procedures. Can be performed under monitored anaesthesia, known as conscious sedation. Cost: from £2600. Lasts indefinitely. | Temporary blurred vision. Possible temporary dry eyes. |

| This is my problem | The Surgery | What should I know | What are the risks? |
|---|---|---|---|
| Heavy brow | Brow-lift | Can be performed through minimal incisions (endobrow). Can be combined with other facial surgery. Can be performed under conscious sedation. Cost: from £1500. May only last one to two years. | Nerve damage can cause temporary paralysis of the brow. Going too far can cause a permanently 'surprised' expression. |
| Big or misshapen nose | Nose job (Rhinoplasty) | Can be performed from inside the nostril (internal scars) or with a small external scar. General anaesthetic required. Cost: from £2800. Lasts indefinitely. | Nasal bleeding is common. Going too far and ending up like Michael Jackson. |
| Chinless wonder | Chin augmentation (Mentoplasty) | A solid implant is stitched to the underlying tissue. Alternative is to manipulate the existing bone, sliding it forward. General anaesthetic required. Cost: from £1200. Lasts indefinitely. | Important to ensure that chin and nose are balanced to create a pleasing profile. |
| BODY<br>Love handles and thunder thighs | Liposuction or Liposculpture | Liposculpture very good for removal of stubborn areas of fat (love handles, pubic region, inner thighs). Will not reduce cellulite. Can be performed under conscious sedation. Cost: from £1500. Lasts indefinitely. | Excess saggy skin will remain if very overweight. Risk of excess fluid build-up. Risk of a fat embolus (clot) in the bloodstream. |
| Saggy arse or Saggy thighs | Buttock-lift or Thigh-lift | Removes excess fat and skin. Good surgery for the right patient. Often done after a massive weight loss. General anaesthetic required. Cost: from £2800. Lasts indefinitely. | Can cause significant scarring and possibly permanent numbness. |
| Flabby tummy | Liposuction with Tummy tuck (Abdominoplasty) | Liposuction removes abdominal fat. Will not remove excess skin where abdominoplasty is required. Can range from mini-abdominoplasty (a smaller operation for a smaller problem) or full abdominoplasty with muscle tightening.General anaesthetic required.Cost: from £2100. Lasts indefinitely. | Will leave a permanent scar. Risk of skin loss (necrosis). Risk of blood clots. |
| Varicose veins | Sclerotherapy | A solution is injected to permanently close off the enlarged blood vessel. No anaesthetic. Can use a localised numbing cream. Cost: from £200. Veins can recur, particularly on the legs. | Can cause bleeding into the skin resulting in discolouration. |

# SHOES THE RULES

## Shapely ankles and calves

Delicate kitten heel shows off a slim ankle to best advantage.

Slim curvy heel echoes the shape of the calf.

Strap draws attention to the elegant ankle.

## Chunky calves with skinny ankles

Backless slippers show off a slim ankle.

A slimmer ankle is flattered by a curved heel while a thicker calf still needs a chunky shoe to balance it.

Sturdy heel balances out the calf while detail on the back of the shoe draws attention to a shapely ankle.

# Chunky calves with no ankles

A chunky straight wedge balances a thicker calf.

Open peep toe lengthens the leg and takes attention away from the ankle.

A stretchy boot covers the size of the calf.

# Short legs

The only flats the short legged should wear, with a very deep cleavage to give full length to the leg.

Lack of any straps creates an unhindered sweep of leg from knee to toe.

Nude colour of the sandal will blend into the flesh and elongate the leg.

June

| | | | |
|---|---|---|---|
| Get your feet ready for summer sandals<br><br>1 | 2 | 3 | 4 |
| 9 | Check the condition of your swimsuits<br><br>10 | 11 | 12 |
| 17 | Give your barbecue equipment a good scrub<br><br>18 | 19 | 20 |
| 25 | 26 | 27 | 28 |

| | | | |
|---|---|---|---|
| Go through your summer wardrobe and write a list of what's missing<br><br>5 | 6 | 7 | 8 |
| 13 | 14 | Buy foreign adaptor plugs<br><br>15 | 16 |
| It's summer — remember to drink more water<br><br>21 | 22 | 23 | 24 |
| 29 | 30 | | |

'Feeling broke? Use reward vouchers to bribe children into doing their chores. When they have all earned one, grant a mutually rewarding treat — extra telly or fish and chips all round.'

# HOW TO MAKE CHILDREN WORSHIP YOU

We love them, but they can be a pain in the backside and the older they get the more the feeling becomes mutual. If you want your little darlings to worship the hallowed ground you walk on, you need to start early. We don't profess to be experts on child rearing, but over the years we have harvested loads of tips from friends and family. We hope some of them will help you too.

## Top tips for coping with kids **0-2**

If your baby is snuffly, lift his mattress at the head end by putting a couple of phone books under the legs of the cot. This will encourage the mucus to drain away.

Cover the top part of the cot with muslin to save stains on sheets. A black-and-white postcard in the cot can be a source of great interest for a baby.

Classical music is good. Make a tape or CD of instrumental 'sleep music'. Play the same music when it's time to go to sleep wherever you are – at home, in the car or in a hotel.

A swaddled baby is a happy baby.

Don't be afraid to make noise when your baby is asleep, though do avoid Motorhead at full volume.

If your baby is crying excessively go into a quiet darkened room to give him a sense of security and no stimulation...it's a bit like a flotation tank.

Babies can easily get over stimulated. Don't feel you always need to be playing with your baby when he's awake.

Give your teething baby a piece of frozen apple to chew on.

Give an anxious or agitated baby a bath, then rub his back with some Vick and use a small soft paintbrush to brush along the spine towards the heart. This is a very effective way of calming a baby.
To get into a good eating routine make sure you start with small portions that aren't just slopped on the plate.
Don't use too many no's and try not to say 'bad', 'naughty' or 'stupid'. Instead try 'We don't do things like that', 'That's not nice' or 'That behaviour is not acceptable'.
Invest in a good bouncy chair.
A wound-down baby sleeps better. Remember bath, book, milk and bed. A good bedtime routine started from the beginning prevents problems later on.
Always be one step ahead of your toddler.

## Top tips for coping with kids **2-6**

Your time, hugs, kisses and praise are more important than any gift.
If your child knows how to do something herself, don't finish it for her just to get it done more quickly.
If they get too many birthday gifts hide half of them in the closet and recycle as rewards throughout the year.
Ask your child to choose one present to give away to charity.
Be a friend but remember you are a parent. Your child expects you to set boundaries.
If you see a tantrum coming practise the art of distraction.
If travelling and you know they are fussy eaters, make sure you bring familiar back-up food if they refuse the local fare.
Get them out of the pushchair from two and a half. Tell them they are far too grown-up to be seen sitting in a pram.
To get rid of dummies invent a 'dummy fairy' at your local toy-shop to whom your rubber sucking angel can give their dummy in exchange for a shiny new toy.
Consistency is imperative. If you threaten a punishment you must carry it out or you will be no more than a liar who doesn't stick to your word. Kids need to be told not to do stuff.

# Top tips for coping with kids 6-12

Put loving and funny notes in their lunchbox and pockets, etc especially when starting full-time school (so they can remember they might be gone but are not forgotten) or some little trinket that will remind them of home.

When you have to travel and leave them behind put little notes around the house for them to find.

Put a surprise in the lunchbox.

Add a marble to an empty glass when they're good and remove one when they're naughty. A full glass earns a reward. Keep the reward on a high shelf so they can see what they're working towards.

Instead of allowing a child to continually creep into bed with you, organise once a month 'Angel nights' for girls and 'Monkey nights' for boys when they are allowed to sleep with mummy and daddy. It's a huge treat.

If your child continually comes into your bedroom in the middle of the night, make up a little 'nest' on the floor so they can be near you but not in your bed.

Make sure their bed is a warm sumptuous haven that seems cosy and inviting.

If you get endless night-time visits bribe them. Five nights in their own bed = present.

Maintain a hierarchy among the children. When they get to certain specified ages they get to do certain things like use grown-up cutlery or re-decorate their rooms. Just because your 10-year-old has a mobile phone doesn't mean the 6-year-old can have one too.

Don't be frightened of your children being bored. You need to let yourself off the hook. Say 'go and tidy your room' and you'll be amazed at how quickly they will find something far more important and urgent to do.

If you are a working mum who isn't able to pick up the kids so often, add to the excitement by putting a sweetie treat on their seat and one for their friend if they have a play date. If their best mate worships you, your child is more likely to as well.

When you need to clear out their room, get them to choose things to get rid of at a car boot sale and let them keep some of the money. Do it collectively as a family.

Avoid war when you switch of the computer or TV by setting an electric timer to the plug. It's not you being mean but the wretched timer... 'sorry guys'.

Set up family email accounts so that all the children's emails are automatically copied to you. Firmly explain that this is not done to spy on them, but so that you can check they are not receiving any inappropriate messages from possibly dangerous strangers. If you're unsure how to do this talk to your internet service provider.

Agree a shorter time for the TV to be on and you can give them an extra 15 minutes so you look like the good guy.

## Top tips for coping with kids 13+

Give them freedom to be themselves and not what you would like them to be

Remember boys grow out of puberty eventually. In the meantime the stage of not washing can be alleviated with a chart for bathing and rewards for a minimum number of baths or showers per week.

Get Net Nanny (www.netnanny.com) for blocking access to inappropriate websites.

When your teenager has done something unacceptable explain what they have done and then ask them 'What do you think? It makes them look at the situation objectively and understand what they have done.

Remember boys of 13+ are just naturally clumsy. Accept that your teenage son is going to break things and stock up on cheap china and glass.

Give a teenager a lock for the inside of her bedroom door.

Embarrass your teenagers into silence by breaking into song when they are demanding everything in the supermarket.

Pay for things for them as much as possible with cash so that they have a more visual idea of the real cost.

Get nametapes with appropriate messages made to sew into your favourite clothes. For example: stolen from my mum.

Teenagers are notorious for pushing your buttons and the boundaries. Put your emotional armour on and be firm. It is not necessary to win every showdown. If the situation becomes too heightened, remove yourself from the scene. They may hate you for being strict. The bonus is that this loathing won't last forever. One day in the far distant future they will thank you.

# HOW TO BE A
# FAIRY GODPARENT

Strictly speaking, the role of the godparent is to guide their godchild in religious and spiritual development. In reality, we usually end up behaving like surrogate cash machines, doling out gifts and readies to assuage a feeling of guilt engendered by providing no spiritual guidance whatsoever.

Don't be afraid to be a godparent. Children love and appreciate your attention. Take your godchildren to a fun park for the entire day. It is a real sacrifice to take a day to schlep around one of these places, but you will be afforded legend like status. Give them your time, patience and attention at times of family stress. If you have several godchildren it's difficult to remember all their birthdays. Instead, give them all a present on your birthday every year. Give them three presents randomly throughout the year, instead of on their birthday or Christmas. Never knowing when their gifts might arrive creates a delicious sense of anticipation. Take them to see your favourite football team play at home (keeps them happy and keeps you happy too!). Expand their minds with thought-provoking books. Do 'grown-up' things with your godchild. Take her to lunch at a fancy restaurant. Go to a gallery and discuss the merits of contemporary art. Taking them to a pop concert will make you their ultimate hero forever. Send souvenirs and cards in the post. For children, receiving post is still very exciting. Also they love stamps from exotic locations. Sponsor a child in another country who was born on the same day, or near enough, as your godchild. Encourage your godchild to send letters and cards. As they grow up together they will develop a lasting interest in each other's lives and cultures. If you ever meet any celebrities or TV personalities ask for a personalised autograph to your godchild. This is guaranteed to impress. Have them round for a sleep over and spoil them rotten. Never undermine their parents. Respect the boundaries that have been set for your godchild. If they're not allowed sweets, so be it. Have personalised gifts made that are special and unique to them. For example a lockable diary with their name embossed on the cover. Send them CDs of obscure music from all over the world. Ask their mother how you can help. Offer to baby-sit occasionally. Take them to church (mosque, temple, etc.)

The
lovely thing
about being a
godparent is that you
get to do a lot of the
fun stuff without ever
having to be the
horrible enforcer
of unfair boring
rules.

# KEEPING KIDS

## On plane, train and car journeys

✳ Count the number of red cars (little kids only).

✳ Make a word from the number-plate letters in the order the letters appear on the plate.

✳ Keep a lap tray in the car with fuzzy felts and magnetic games at hand to play with.

✳ Where are the lorries from? Which country? Which town?

✳ A to Z – starting with the youngest to oldest, everyone thinks of an animal starting with the letter A, and moves onto B and so on down the alphabet. Finished? Move on to countries.

✳ Who am I? Someone thinks of a famous person and everyone else asks a question in turn that can only have a yes or no answer.

# ENTERTAINED

* **Capital cities – parents say a country and children say the capital and vice versa.**

* Talking tapes for any age.

* **Mobile scavenger hunt – make a list before the journey and see who spots the most things from the list.**

* I packed in my bag and in my bag I packed. A go-round where each person adds an imaginary item to the imaginary bag, increasing the contents, and then has to remember and recite the entire contents of the bag.

* Educate them in your musical tastes.

* **Sweet and sour – wave to passers-by. If they wave back it's sweet, if not the kids can stick out their tongues.**

* Bring the most delicious picnic and have a feast en-route.

# On a sunny Saturday

* **Hold a garden fete – the kids will spend hours creating tombolas, raffles, coconut shies and cake stalls.**

* Follow a fairy trail – make an original fairy note that leads to clues around the garden or park. Only the fairy interpreter (mummy) can read the fairy messages that are written in the leaves, shadows, moss and pebbles. The trail ends in a delicious meal which the fairy has left (fairies love salad and green vegetables).

* **Get them to make something to sell on the street – lemonade, baked goods, little plants or fresh herbs. The proceeds will go to their favourite charity, but they will get to keep a percentage of the profits. Keep an eye on them to make sure they don't start**
  **a. Flagging down strangers in passing cars or**
  **b. Becoming budding Alan Sugars and selling off all the family silver at 10p a piece.**

* Create a treasure hunt by hiding their small toys around the garden.

* **Give the kids a little area of the garden that is theirs alone. Encourage them to grow plants, set up a campsite and have picnics. You are not allowed into the private garden without the secret password.**

* If you have a big garden get the kids to build a crazy-golf course. Holes are made from plastic flowerpots sunk into the lawn. Obstacles can include bits of pipe, squares of carpet, ramps made of boards and bricks, and plants in pots. Use plastic golf clubs and balls.

* **Building a compost heap will turn your kids into budding worm farmers.**

* The RSPB's Pocket Birds is exactly what it says – a portable book full of descriptions and photographs of over 300 common birds. Perfect for country walks.

* **Encourage the children to observe the universe on clear nights. You can download and print out a map of the stars from: www.fourmilab.ch/yoursky**

# On a rainy Sunday

✳ Keep them active by building an indoor obstacle course.

✳ Kids love cooking and making lotions and potions. These could include flower waters, body lotions (made by adding essential oils to Nivea) or exotic fruit 'cocktails'.

✳ Organise an indoor scavenger hunt. Think of fun, simple things to find: a cobweb, a feather, a sock, a napkin, a key.

✳ Run and find. Run and find something beginning with A, then run back to mummy. Run and find something beginning with B...

✳ Assemble an assortment of peculiar ingredients and challenge the kids to make innovative sandwiches from them. Cover the table with newspaper and have an indoor picnic.

✳ BE US is a fabulous game where the children play the role of parents and the parents become children. It's enormous fun and gives revealing insights into how your children perceive you. Expect to be scolded, bossed around and forced to eat a few revolting monstrosities. When you end up in the bath with your husband having your necks scrubbed, you know it's been a triumph.

✳ Learn a new board game.

✳ Twister is a perennial favourite.

✳ Get involved in one of their computer games.

✳ If you have a gang of friends in the house, put the names of all the children into a hat. They each draw out a name in turn and then dress up and act like the person they have picked. This can also be done with the names of celebrities or fictional characters.

✳ Take them to an art gallery. Give them art materials and ask them to find their favourite painting, then get them to sit down and create their own version of the painting.

✳ Designate a creative wall in the bedroom where they are allowed to draw, do graffiti, make collages, stick stickers, etc.

✳ Always keep a dressing-up box of your old cast-offs.

# PATTERN & TEXTURE THE RULES

## Sequin

Use a plain base to layer a sequin top and skirt. Glass jewellery contrasts with the sequin appliqué.

Only ever layer chiffon appliqué and sequins if the base colours are the same. Choose sequins in the same colour as the skirt.

## Black & White

Make sure you wear the darkest colour from a stripe to flatter your bottom half.

Wear a necklace in the darkest colour to balance out the darkness of the skirt.

## Textures

Choose the brightest colour from the textured tweed coat for the top and the darker shade for the trousers.

Choose a colour that works for you and wear it in different textures. Combining tweed, satin, sequin and glass beads adds richness.

# Bold colour    Print on plain    Print on print

Enrich bright colours with white rather than black. Bring the white back into the top half with a necklace of the same colour.

Choose the most neutral colour from a printed top as your skirt colour. Use a wide belt to bring together print and plain garments.

When clashing prints together, at least two of the colours need to match. Add a plain top or bottom so the outfit is not too chaotic.

Balance the strong colour of the top by toning it with a similarly coloured plain skirt and keep the jewellery in the same tones.

Take the brightest colour from the skirt for the top. Wear jewellery in the darkest shade to balance the brightness of the top

The prints should be different shades of the same colour. The plain colour you choose to offset the print should be in the darkest shade.

# PATTERN & TEXTURE

## DO

Experiment with items in your existing wardrobe that you have been scared of wearing.

Madly match them with a similar item. Then go out to get a reaction from your friends and see how it makes you feel.

Wear small prints if you are delicate and petite, and big prints if you are tall and bold.

If you are top heavy and wearing a pattern on your bottom, choose the darkest colour from that print for your top half.

If you are pear shaped and wearing the pattern on your bottom half, choose the lightest shade from that print for your top half.

Wear texture on your smaller half only. Avoid texture that bulks you up.

Consider mixing luxury and daytime fabrics – velvet trousers and a cool plain T-shirt.

Wear patterns together so long as the colour palette comes from the same family and is in colours that suit you.

You can wear big bold jewellery with a strong pattern as long as it includes a colour from the pattern.

## DON'T

Wear a print if you can visualise it as a soft furnishing.

Mix too many floral designs together – you will look like a garden.

Be afraid to wear silver with gold rather than silver with silver. It's more individual.

Wear velvet top and bottom.

Wear denim with denim.

Wear same-size patterns; small and big together is better.

Wear a brightly patterned top with black trousers.

Wear leather on your bottom half. Never wear a leather jacket and trousers, even Kate Moss couldn't get away with it.

Wear lace or crochet on big tits.

Wear trousers in flimsy fabrics like satin or silk crepe if you suffer from cellulite. Every judder will show.

Be afraid to sparkle in the daytime.

Wear sequinned jeans with sparkly tops. It's too much.

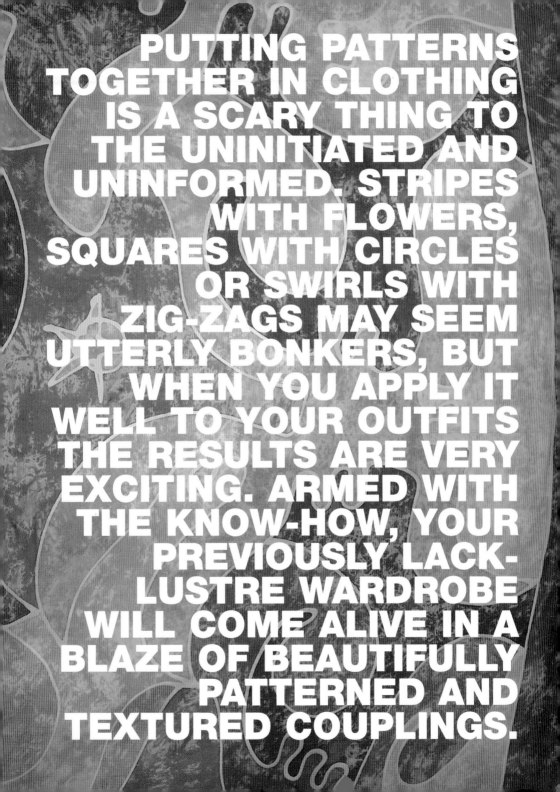

PUTTING PATTERNS TOGETHER IN CLOTHING IS A SCARY THING TO THE UNINITIATED AND UNINFORMED. STRIPES WITH FLOWERS, SQUARES WITH CIRCLES OR SWIRLS WITH ZIG-ZAGS MAY SEEM UTTERLY BONKERS, BUT WHEN YOU APPLY IT WELL TO YOUR OUTFITS THE RESULTS ARE VERY EXCITING. ARMED WITH THE KNOW-HOW, YOUR PREVIOUSLY LACK-LUSTRE WARDROBE WILL COME ALIVE IN A BLAZE OF BEAUTIFULLY PATTERNED AND TEXTURED COUPLINGS.

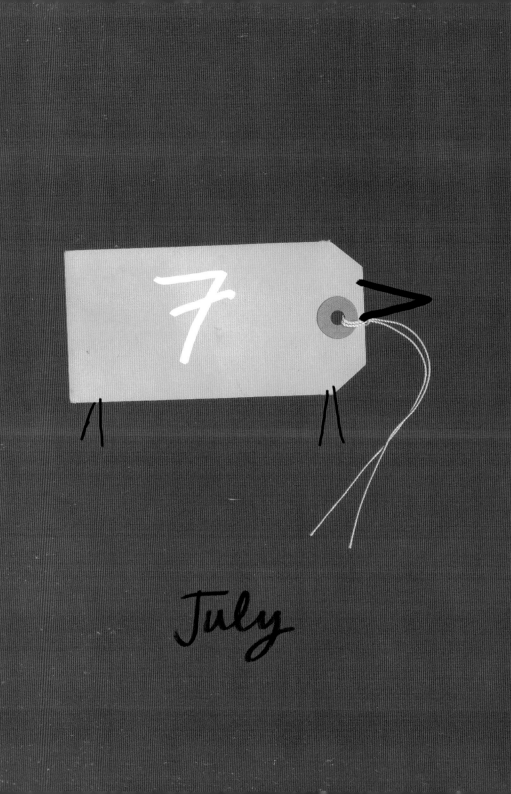

July

| | | | |
|---|---|---|---|
| Summer sales start<br><br><br>1 | <br><br><br>2 | <br><br><br>3 | Have your eyelashes tinted<br><br><br>4 |
| <br><br><br>9 | Get a bikini wax<br><br><br>10 | <br><br><br>11 | <br><br><br>12 |
| Check home security before going away<br><br><br>17 | <br><br><br>18 | <br><br><br>19 | <br><br><br>20 |
| <br><br><br>25 | <br><br><br>26 | <br><br><br>27 | Stock up on holiday reading<br><br><br>28 |

JULY

| | | | |
|---|---|---|---|
| Book your summer holiday haircut | | | |
| 5 | 6 | 7 | 8 |
| | Stock up on sunscreen, citronella, calamine lotion etc | | |
| 13 | 14 | 15 | 16 |
| 21 | 22 | 23 | 24 |
| 29 | 30 | 31 | |

'Beach aside, if you are over 40 wear shorts that end at the knee, not above.'

*for a two week holiday*

- 5 bikinis (if not more as they are always wet, crusty in the gusset and you wear them all day long)

- 5 sarongs (2 with sparkle to double up as skirts)

- 5 dresses

- 3 T-shirts/vests

- 4 fun tops

- 2 skirts

- 1 pair of gold or silver flat sandals

- 1 pair flip-flops or Birkenstocks

- 3 G-strings (easy to wash)

- Gold hoop earrings

- Silver hoop earrings

- 2 bras

- 1 light sweater

- 2 long kaftans (for beach and slouchy evenings in)

- Hat

- 2 pairs of sunglasses

# PACK CLEVER

## PRE-TEENAGE GIRL

*for a two week holiday*

- 3–5 swimsuits/bikinis
- 7 pairs of knickers (girls like variety; give it to them in something that takes up little room)
- 5 tops (2 that double up as sun protectors and 3 to feel pretty)
- 1 sweater or towelling dress (girls like to feel snuggly after a long time in the water)
- 1 pair of shorts or 2 sarongs
- 2 skirts (to work with tops)
- 4 dresses/kaftans
- 1 pair of sandals (make them sturdy as well as pretty so they can multi-purpose)
- 2 long nightdresses or PJs (to keep off the mozzies)
- 1 hat
- 1 pair of sunglasses (these can be fun to buy on site, especially as they will be lost or broken by the end of the holiday)
- 2–4 bottles of sunscreen (allow 1 to 2 bottles a week per child)
- Toothbrush

## PRE-TEENAGE BOY

*for a two week holiday*

- 3–5 pairs of swimming trunks (they are in the water all day)
- 3 pairs of knickers (can be easily and cheaply washed)
- 5 T-shirts (more than enough to feel a change in outfit)
- 1 sweater (for aeroplane and cloudy days)
- 2 pairs of shorts
- 2 pairs of trousers
- 1 pair of beach type shoes (flip-flops or surf shoes for hot sand)
- 1 pair of trainers or Birkenstocks – will do for all occasions
- 2 pairs of pyjamas (long and light predominantly to keep off mosquitoes)
- 1 hat
- 2 bottles of sunscreen
- Toothbrush

# PACKING LISTS:

I mustn't forget to take:

Passport

Tickets

Bank cards

Driving licence

Cash

'I'm always highly
organised before I go.
Every inch of my suitcase
is packed with precision.'

## nappies

**Susannah's way**
Take nappies to last a couple of days. They take up too much room in a suitcase and are widely available abroad.

**Trinny's way**
Take the exact number of nappies you'll need for the trip. The space they vacate can be filled up with shopping!

# packing for kids

When packing for your children (assuming they are still of an age when they are happy for you to do it) don't you find you take too much... or too little? Those with multiple siblings, like us, will certainly appreciate the challenge of taking as little as possible. The key to sticking to this good intention is to not get swept away by how adorable they look in this, that or the other. Susannah's band of banshees are still quite happy to wear next to nothing on a beach holiday and don't realise that they have worn the same dress or T-shirt 3 nights in a row, just so long as it is one of their favourites.

## FOR ALL

Toothpaste
Citronella as insect repellent
Calpol or any other kiddie fever remedy
Rescue Remedy (to calm tears after a fright)
Arnica (for bumps and bruises)
Antihistamine cream
Hairbrush

# COPING WITH KIDS ON AEROPLANES

If you have more than one child, flying, especially those long haul buggers, can be pure hell. It is vital that you take your own in-flight entertainment and select treats to hold the kids hostage.

## COMFORT

- Pashminas for softness and warmth

- Small bottles of water

- Phenegan (a drowsy-making antihistamine for kids) to knock them out on night flights only. NB: test it out first because some children can become hyperactive... not ideal in the confines of economy where there is no room to fart let alone swing from the overhead lockers.

# games

- Magnetic Snakes & Ladders
- Draughts
- Noughts and Crosses
- Top Trumps
- Colours & paper
- Fuzzy Felt (it sticks)
- Talking books
- Portable CD player

## Bribes

Lollipops for take off and landing •

Yoghurt-coated raisins •

Smarties to play counting games with •

+ = HAPPY FLIGHT

# SURVIVING

## THE LONG HAUL

**Modern air travel is more a gruelling ordeal than a glamorous adventure. The best we can hope for is to endure it without feeling like we want to bail out over the Indian Ocean.**

### Try for the upgrade
The insanity of marketing has lead some airlines to introduce FOUR classes of travel. It's always worth trying to get pushed up to the one above. Apart from extra legroom just the pure sweet satisfaction of getting something for nothing can take much of the pain out of sitting for twelve hours. Dress well (but comfortably), smile sweetly and ask reasonably. Throwing a strop will get you nowhere.

### One class
The best alternative is to travel on an airline that offers only one class of service. That way at least you feel you're all in the same boat.

### Personal space
Once wedged aboard, make the most of it. A lot of the stress is caused by the feeling of people encroaching into your personal space. Make your seat into a little home. Plan what you will need during the flight and make sure that it's all accessible.

### Heavenly smells
Like cats, we spray our seat before settling in, using a lavender and tea-tree spray that kills germs and smells heavenly.

**CHILL OUT** Once seated we take off our shoes, don our anti-thrombosis socks (these are not a luxury but an essential item), clean our faces, slather on some moisturiser, down a multi-vitamin, wrap our bodies in a big shawl, insert ear plugs, pull on a sleep mask and hunker down for the duration.

# In-flight kit

Wool or cashmere shawl

Rescue Remedy

Night cream

Multi-vitamins

Mineral water

Baby pillow

Anti-DVT socks

Apis homeopathic pills

Deodorant wipes

Pillow spray

Mini toothpaste and brush

iPod

Earplugs

Eye masks

# 'We want to protect ourselves, and our children, from sunburn and the possibility of developing skin cancer but the information is so confusing.'

We've had a chat with Cancer Research UK and here's what we learned.

**THE BEST WAY TO AVOID SUNBURN** and skin cancer is to stay out of the sun as much as possible. Wear a hat and a long-sleeved shirt. Take a big umbrella to the beach or park. Wear good sunglasses, especially wraparounds.

THE SUN SHINES not only at the beach. Get into the habit of using protection every day for work, school and play.

PROTECT CHILDREN This is especially important – 80% of sun exposure occurs before the age of 18.

# SUN SAFETY

## WHAT DOES SUNSCREEN DO?

Chemical sunscreens absorb the sun's rays. The only chemical ingredient currently believed to protect against UVA is Avobenzone (or Parsol 1789). But it doesn't protect against UVB so it needs to be combined with another chemical sunscreen – titanium dioxide.

Non-chemical sunblocks deflect the sun's rays. Titanium dioxide gives some protection against UVA and considerable protection against UVB.

Zinc oxide is the most effective protection against UVA and UVB. Zinc oxide sunscreens used to be gunky and white but now they are lighter and more transparent.

# How is sunlight harmful?

There are two types of harmful sun radiation: UVB, which causes sunburn, and the more dangerous UVA, which penetrates deep into the skin and is thought to be responsible for malignant melanomas.

## USING SUNSCREEN

Apply early – about 20 minutes before you go into the sun to give it time to start working.

Don't be stingy – you need a big handful (50 grams) to cover your body. Three-quarters of a handful for a child.

Be thorough – cover your back, your neck, your wrists, under the straps of your swimsuit and the bottoms of your feet (if you're lying in the sun).

Don't be lazy – reapply the same amount every two hours.

A water-resistant sunscreen will give you about 40 minutes of protection in the water or playing tennis. Apply more sunscreen after you have dried off with a towel.

If there is no expiry date, write the purchase date on the label in felt-tip pen and throw it away when it's two years old. It deteriorates with time.

## WHAT IS SPF?

Sun Protection Factor refers to how much the sunscreen protects against UVB only. The paler your skin, the higher SPF you must use. Everyone, even those with dark skin, should use at least SPF15. Lower than that is close to useless. Be aware that using SPF30 (97% UBV protection) does not mean you can stay in the sun twice as long as if you used SPF15 (93% UBV protection). All sunscreens with an SPF number protect from UVB but it is most important to look for a preparation that protects from UVA as well. These are often labelled 'broad spectrum'.

## Our favourite brand

is ZO1 – SPF30. It contains zinc for maximum UVB and UVA protection but it rubs in and does not leave us looking like petrified chalk women.

**Forget to pack your first aid kit? Our friends at the British Red Cross have some advice on how you can use what might be to hand in a medical emergency.**

# MEDICAL EMERGENCIES

## chocolate for a diabetic

Giving chocolate to a conscious diabetic who is having a hypoglycaemia attack will help raise the blood sugar level. You can also give chocolate to someone with hypothermia as a high-energy food will help to warm the body.

## lose a tooth? put it in milk

If an adult tooth is knocked out and cannot be put back in its socket, it should be placed in a container of milk to stop it drying out. This will increase the possibility of it being successfully replanted by a dental surgeon.

## paper bag for a panic attack

A panic attack can often result in hyperventilation. Get the sufferer to breathe into a paper bag which will help to regulate and slow down the breathing.

## tepid water to remove an insect from the ear

If someone gets an insect in the ear, do not rub the area as it will push the creature further in. Sit the person down and support the head so that the affected ear is uppermost. Then gently flood the ear with tepid water from a tumbler and the insect will float out. If this does not work, go to casualty.

## sheet to help heatstroke

Heatstroke is caused by too much time in the sun. The body temperature rises above 40°C (104°F) causing headache, dizziness and disorientation. Move the sufferer into the shade, take off as much outer clothing as possible and then wrap the whole body in a cold, wet sheet. Keep the sheet wet until the body temperature falls below 37.5°C (99.5°F). You can then replace the wet sheet with a dry one. Keep checking the body temperature. Note: this is an adult treatment only.

### credit card to remove a sting

If an insect sting is visible on the skin, use the edge of a credit card (or the back of a butter knife or similarly slim, stiff object) to scrape it away. It's better than using a pair of tweezers as some stings contain a sac of poison that ruptures if grasped with tweezers.

### beer or iced water for a burn

To treat a burn or scald, act immediately to cool the burnt area. Beer, soft drink, milk or any other cold liquid can be used to cool the burn while finding a supply of cold running water. If you have a cooler full of iced water, submerge the burn completely for at least 10 minutes to make sure the treatment is effective.

## pair of tights for a fracture

Collarbone fractures are common among children. They are usually caused by falling onto an outstretched hand. Use a pair of tights (or a belt or tie) as an improvised support. Put the tights around the neck and tie in a figure of eight. Place the hand in the bottom loop at chest level on the uninjured side of the body, just below the shoulder. Check for circulation in the arm by pressing on the fingernail bed, which will initially turn white and then should return to its normal colour in a few seconds. If it doesn't, you need to re-do the sling so that it is not so tight.

### jumper for an arm injury

A wrist or lower arm injury needs to be supported with a sling. If you don't have a square scarf or sarong to hand, use a long-sleeved T-shirt or jumper. Support the injured arm on the body of the jumper placing the hand at the neck end. Tie the sleeves around the neck so that the arm is roughly at a 90° angle. Use a safety pin to close the sling at the elbow to stabilise the injury and reduce the pain. Make sure you leave the fingers exposed in order to continue to check the circulation to the arm (as above).

# ESSENTIAL HOLIDAY TIPS

**HERE'S HOW YOU CAN TURN YOUR HOTEL INTO A HOME AWAY FROM HOME...**

Photos of loved ones left behind in a compact folding frame. **Your favourite bath oil.** A travel-sized scented candle. **Your own favourite soap.** Wax earplugs to block out noisy neighbours and partying teenagers. **A soft baby pillow with a cotton pillowslip.** A travel alarm clock. **Take at least one international adapter plug. Hotels NEVER have them and they are impossible to find once you reach your destination.** It's so much more relaxing to travel by train than by car or plane. It's more environmentally friendly too! Treat the extra time it takes as a part of your holiday. A sleeper train journey is great fun for kids, romantic for couples and a wonderful time to read and think if you're travelling alone. **Bring along your own CDs for your rental car. Count the number of cases you have every time you check in/out, load the car, etc.** Remember that you're on holiday to unwind, not undertake a Napoleonic rampage across Europe. Schedule only one outing per day and leave at least one day a week free to do absolutely nothing. **It might seem sensible to save an extra night's hotel charges by flying home overnight but the toll it takes on your body will leave you feeling like you need another holiday to recover. Take a daytime flight at the end of the holiday. You'll arrive home just in time to go to bed so sleep patterns will get back to normal that much more quickly.**

+

+

=

# HOME SWEET HOME

# SWIMWEAR THE RULES

## Big tits

Choose a balcony bra
for total support and lift.

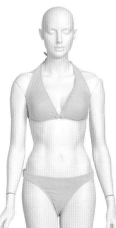

For saggy, larger breasts go for a
halter neck to give a better cleavage.

Make sure your swimsuit has hidden
cups for extra support.

## No tits

A halter-neck bra top with padding
will pull together what cleavage you
may have, or create one where there
isn't anything of note.

If your tummy is your better asset,
then put all the focus
on the abs.

The width of the halter-neck
balances out the lack of breasts and
the detailed stitching gives the figure
more shape.

# Flabby tummy

The ruching and belt detail give a nipped-in waist and cover tummy flab.

A strategically placed short sarong will hide a flabby tummy without shortening the legs.

The tankini allows you to get your tummy brown...and control when it is on show.

# Saddlebags

A string-tie bikini is the most flattering as there is less fabric to cut into the width of the saddlebags.

The wide horizontal line helps to balance the width of the hips. A high-cut leg draws the eye up and away from the saddlebags.

Use a pareo to cover up one side of your saddlebags and tie on the other to draw attention away from the area.

August

Calam
lotion

| | | | |
|---|---|---|---|
| Reload your iPod with new tunes | | | |
| 1 | 2 | 3 | 4 |
| | | | Send postcards to people you haven't seen in ages |
| 9 | 10 | 11 | 12 |
| 17 | 18 | 19 | 20 |
| Get your central heating checked | | | |
| 25 | 26 | 27 | 28 |

AUGUST

| 5 | 6 | 7 | 8 |
|---|---|---|---|
| | | Stock up on cards while on holiday | |
| 13 | 14 | 15 | 16 |
| 21 | 22 | 23 | 24 |
| 29 | 30 | 31 | |
| | Wash and dry all your swimsuits and store them away in ziplock bags | | |

'Put aside a "helping hour" once a week when the whole family pitches in. Many hands make light work.'

# GET MORE TIME OUT OF YOUR DAY

## The night before

**Exfoliate and shave the night before so you only need a shower.**

**Make sure your bag is filled and ready so you are not hunting around for your wallet and diary at the last minute.**

**Don't forget the car you left parked on a yellow line. Get up early and move your car first thing in the morning.**

If you haven't got a public transport pass make sure you have coins.

**Always put your keys back in the same place. Create a place near the front door (which cannot be seen or reached through the letterbox) for a key rack or bowl.**

Charge your mobile phone overnight.

**Lay your clothes out the night before. The outfit you put out last night and hate this morning? You haven't put weight on overnight, it still looks good: WEAR IT.**

Make sure the kids have laid out their own school uniforms.

**If you aspire to drinking hot water and lemon in the morning but never get around to it, put it in a thermos the night before. Or prepare your favourite beverage the night before so all you have to do is add the boiling water.**

If you are going somewhere new, make sure you plot your route the night before.

In the morning
there are any number of
things that can hold you back
from a speedy exit, be it
'I've got nothing to wear',
'I feel ghastly' or 'Where are
my sodding keys?'

This is how we do it...

# Every month or two

Put together lots of different outfits for various occasions using the clothes and accessories in your wardrobe. Polaroid yourself wearing them, then stick the photos inside your cupboard door. This will make it easy to choose outfits when you haven't got much time.

**Make lists of what's in your freezer, bathroom cabinet, kitchen cupboards, etc., so it's easy to see what you need to stock up on when it's time to replenish at the supermarket.**

Go to the bank and get £50 in £1 coins so you never run out of change.

Have your nails professionally tipped in polish that will last a month to avoid the chipped nail-syndrome panic.

**Get your eyelashes permed and dyed to save the time taken up with eyelash curlers and mascara.**

If you spend hours on straightening your hair with flat irons consider getting it professionally straightened. It should last a few months.

Once a month have a big cook-up of soups and stews and freeze in double portions for those emergency moments when you can't bear yet another takeaway.

What's in the freezer?

Things I need from the chemist

Store cupboard staples

'I am always writing lists. It's the only way I can stay on top of everything that needs to be done.'

# HANGOVER CURE

If you know you are going to have a late one, prepare for the pain by taking two Aspirin (and it can only be Aspirin) before you go out and two more before you go to bed, along with a Berocca in water. Take some almonds with you to eat on the way. They line the stomach. This simple formula will help to cushion the pain of a throbbing hangover. For bloodshot eyes, use Eyedew. Eat a handful of parsley stalks in the morning to take away your dragon's breath.

# Quick beauty fixes

### TIRED FACE
Use an exfoliator like Jason Vita-C Max One Minute Facial to wake up your face. Every few days put some live yogurt on your face for 5–10 minutes while you take a bath for soft, rejuvenated skin.

### MAKING YOUR MAKE-UP LAST
While the bath is running, cleanse your face and put on your make-up (the day you don't need to do the mask) and get in the bath. The steam from the bath will set your make-up for the day.

### PERSPIRATION MARKS
A slice of lemon rubbed onto your armpits will help prevent perspiration marks on your clothes.

### DEODORANT STAINS
Have you put on your favourite dress too soon after your bath and found deodorant marks under the arms? Take a damp (not white) flannel and rub down, then use a hairdryer if needed to dry out the damp patches.

### DIRTY HAIR
A beauty lift for those days when you don't have time to wash your hair is to wear a funky headband in silver or gold. It will lift your features as well as disguise your overly greasy hair. Alternatively, use a dry shampoo like Kevin Murphy Fresh Hair.

### PUFFY EYES AND BAGS
Apply either Preparation H haemorrhoid cream or Dr Sebagh's Puffy Eye Cream as a thick mask for 5 minutes to reduce puffy eyes.

### SPOTS
Jan Marini makes an amazing acne gel. Apply overnight to see a reduced spot in the morning.

## OLD MAKE-UP
Have Q-tips ready to get off your night-before panda eyes.

## PARTY FACE
For that instant glow, our favourite pre-party treat is Dr Sebagh's Deep Exfoliating Mask. www.drsebagh.com

## TAKE AWAY THE SHINE
For a smooth, non-cakey face, use Benefit's Dr Feelgood on your T-zone. It smoothes pores and fine lines and takes away the shine. www.benefitcosmetics.co.uk

## HAND CREAM
Keep a pot of hand cream by the bed. Your hands are the most telling sign of your age.

## A CLOSE SHAVE
If you run out of shaving foam, use olive oil or talcum powder. They give just as good a shave.

# GOOD USE OF TRAVEL TIME

**LEARN A LANGUAGE** Be it one you vaguely know or a brand new one.

**EDUCATE YOURSELF** An introduction to the classics, historical biographies, or any subject of interest.

**LOSE WEIGHT** Paul McKenna's *Think Thin* is a great way to get started.

**STOP SMOKING** Hypnosis tapes can help you to stop smoking.

**BUILD UP YOUR CONFIDENCE** Anthony Robbins *Awaken the Giant Within* is a good start.

**IMPROVE YOUR MEMORY** Enhancing techniques will keep you organised.

**SINGING** It's a great stress buster...

**CATCH UP WITH THE NEWS** Download your favourite podcast radio programme to listen to in your own time.

**AFFIRMATIONS** Record your own or use someone else's.

**THANK YOU NOTES** Write all those letters you are late sending.

**WRITE YOUR JOURNAL** Or a novel, or poetry – use the journey as a creative space.

Here are some ideas for what you can do in the dead time spent travelling in the car, bus or train. So put away the daily news and do something that's going to help you.

ALLEN CARR'S EASY WAY TO STOP SMOKING

CD13 ENERGY & MOTIVATION - By Glenn Ha

SELFHELP THE CONFIDENCE PLAN Sarah Litvinoff

101 POWER THOUGHTS Louise

PAULO COELHO THE ALCHEMIST

PAULO COELHO THE ALCHEMIST

OVERCOMING PHOBIAS

ANTHONY ROBBINS AWAKEN THE GIANT WITHIN

CD07 BUILD YOUR SELF ESTEEM - By Glenn Ha

LOUISE L. HAY Self-Healing

You Can Heal Your Life Louise L.

2-HOUR INTRODUCTORY CD PACK FRENCH WITH Michel Thomas

# KIT FOR THE CAR

Tissues **Cream blusher** Lip gloss in neutral shade **Lavender aromatherapy roll-on to de-stress** Rescue Remedy **Throwaway camera for great sights or recording a car accident** Wet wipes **Bottles of water** Hand cream **Shoes for driving in so you don't scuff up all your expensive heels** £1 coins **Pen and paper for writing notes to the warden** A comb **Packet of dried fruit and almonds for snacking on instead of tempting chocolate** A clear plastic container to keep it all in.

# and when you're
# by yourself in the car...

**Whiten your teeth**
using bleaching trays.
Try Superdrug's own brand
Go Smile.

**Tone your tummy**
Slender tone – tone your
bottom, stomach and thighs
as you drive.

**Soften your hands**
Smother your hands in a hand mask,
put on an old pair of gloves and feel
them soften.

**Flush out toxins**
It's a great time to get in the habit of
drinking water. Set yourself a daily
quota and build up to it.

**Tone your face**
Do your daily facial exercises.
Then take a good look around to
see which of the other drivers are
staring at you.

**Keep your fanny tight**
Pelvic floor exercises are not just
important for women who have
recently had babies but vital for a
good sex life. CAN BE DONE
ANYWHERE.

# JEWELLERY THE RULES

## Big boned

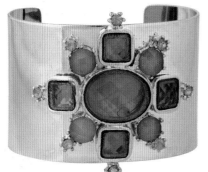

A large cuff is all that's needed to add chic to a Little Black Dress.

Bring attention to your expressive hands with a big bold ring.

Wearing a long, bold necklace in a complementary colour enlivens a simple jumper.

## Slim boned

Delicate multi-faceted gems look best with little bones.

Slim-boned girls can wear long beads if they are uneven in size.

A delicate bracelet doesn't overpower a slim wrist.

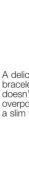

# Short neck

A big brooch can be a great alternative to a large necklace. It will draw attention away from the neck.

Small, dangly earrings give a sense of length to the neck without being overpowering.

Choose a dropped neckline necklace to elongate the neck area.

# Long neck

Show off your long neck by wearing a pair of earrings that would come down to most people's tits (and no other jewellery!).

Shorten a too-long neck with a wide choker.

september

| | | | |
|---|---|---|---|
| 1 | 2 | Write a list of the clothes you actually wore on holiday so you remember what to pack next year<br><br>3 | 4 |
| Think about ideas for half-term<br><br>9 | 10 | 11 | 12 |
| 17 | 18 | Get your chimney swept and check smoke alarms<br><br>19 | 20 |
| 25 | 26 | 27 | 28 |

# SEPTEMBER

| | | | |
|---|---|---|---|
| | | Have your children's feet measured | |
| 5 | 6 | 7 | 8 |
| | | | |
| 13 | 14 | 15 | 16 |
| Have a dyeing session to renew last summer's tired white shirts and T-shirts | | | |
| 21 | 22 | 23 | 24 |
| | Unpack and polish winter shoes | | |
| 29 | 30 | | |

'Your local parish newsletter is born from a trusty community so it's a great resource for extra help, things for sale and household services.'

## Don't stop to think about it

Grab a piece of paper and list your wildest dreams. Allow yourself total freedom. If you find yourself thinking 'that's ridiculous' or 'I couldn't do that' just write it down anyway. Once you have finished writing put your list away for a week and then read it with fresh eyes. Patterns will emerge. You may see that most of your dreams revolve around caring for others, the creative arts or academic pursuits. This process will help to give you insight into what areas of life really inspire you.

## What would you do for a living if training, pay and circumstances were no issue?

## Take a big scrap book

and a pile of old magazines and newspapers. They don't have to be glamorous glossy magazines, Sunday supplements and the local paper will provide ample material. You'll also need scissors and glue. Start flicking through the magazines and tearing out words and images that strike a chord with your visions for different parts of your life. If you desire to own a dog you might come across a photo of a gorgeous puppy. Tear it out and stick it in your dream scrapbook. A swanky house with a rose garden? No problem, the images will be there. Have fun tearing out words and making up headlines for your pages, for example, 'TriNNy is FIRST WOMAN on mARS'. Pick out the most inspiring collages from your scrapbook and have them framed.

# MAKE TIME FOR YOUR DREAMS

ballet dancer, fighter pilot, fashion designer, mother, painter, poet, architect, accountant, interior designer, photographer, catwalk model, inventor, yoga teacher, chef, train driver, chocolatier, nursery teacher, rocket scientist, perfume tester, farmer, forensic scientist, madam, trapeze artist, florist, poker player, stockbroker, editor, archaeologist, lion tamer, tv presenter, meteorologist, explorer, lawyer, astronaut, historian, nurse, masseuse, physiotherapist, croupier, psychic medium, landscape gardener, soldier, schoolteacher, plastic surgeon, housekeeper, fire fighter, gymnast, football coach, sculptor, shop owner, computer engineer, aromatherapist, healer, accordion player, marine biologist, taxi driver, drugs counsellor, prime minister, clown, carpenter, anthropologist, graphic artist.

# Write out your visions

What is your vision for your life?
It's possible that you've buried it so deep
under the necessities of daily existence
that you can barely whisper it. Take a new
notebook and begin to write about your
dream. Do it in the present tense, as if it's
really happening now: 'My husband and
daughter and I are living in a big sunny flat.
The kitchen tiles are yellow and a bunch of
daffodils nod brightly on the windowsill.
Each morning after Jessica has gone to
school I sit at my oak table with coffee and
laptop writing poetry. Sometimes I just stare
into space and then it all comes bursting out
as my fingers fly...' or 'Blades of grass quiver
and flatten silently all around me. Then a
roaring hits my ears as the stick shudders
beneath my hand. I give a thumbs up to my
co-pilot and lift the chopper smoothly to
treetop level...' You get the idea.

# MY VISION:

Write down in your journal what you've achieved
so far in your life. You are a valuable person already.

# MAKING THE TIME

The secret is to set aside an amount of time for your vision that is regular and achievable. Can you find 15 minutes a day to practise your vocal scales? An hour a week to work on your interior design sketches? It doesn't matter how small the amount of time is to start with. The important thing is to stick to it. Be aware that allocating an amount of time that you cannot realistically fulfil is setting yourself up for failure. Don't skip your commitment to yourself and then try to 'catch it up later'.

## Gain the time for your commitment by setting the alarm clock to wake you an hour or even half an hour earlier each day.

## Making the space

There's probably an area in your home specifically designated for cooking (the kitchen), sleeping (the bed), storing old junk (the garden, attic, laundry, hall cupboard, under the bed) and loads of space allocated for watching TV. Give your vision the space it deserves. A clear desk, a painting area, a pinboard for your ideas. The space may be small but it will be dedicated to you, unencumbered by other people's clutter.

## Organise a spiritual spring clean

Thoroughly go through all your possessions touching each one in turn. If you don't love it and you haven't used it for a full year, then it has no place in your life. Sell it, donate it, burn it – just don't allow it to live another minute rent-free in your house. Soon you will be living in a home where everything you see and touch is useful, beautiful and wanted.

# ASKING FOR
## HELP

**Before doing something that fills you with dread and trepidation, pick up the phone to someone else in your group. 'Hello, it's me. I'm just about to propose to my boss that I work one less day a week. I'm feeling a bit sick at the prospect. Wish me luck. I'll call you when I've done it.'**

**30 minutes later. 'Hi, it's me. I had the meeting and she said yes immediately. I didn't realise that she valued my skills so highly.'**

**It's called bookending. Call one of your supporters before taking any difficult steps to discuss what you're about to do. Call afterwards to check in and let them know what you achieved.**

# SETTING UP A
# PRESSURE
# GROUP

## Work together
You're not the only one with
secretly suppressed ambitions.
Get together with a group of friends
and arrange a regular meeting to
support and encourage
one another.

## Let everyone have a say
In the group meeting, allot time for
each person to speak. Talk about
your visions and the practical steps
you are taking to make them
happen. Be specific.

## Follow up
Check in with all your 'groupies' by
email once a week (say, on a Sunday)
to update one another with how
you're getting on. Your email will be
most useful to help keep you
focused, so again be specific and try
to include statements of your
intentions and declarations of
your achievements.

## Use your email
This is an incredibly powerful way
to get the encouragement and
commitment you need to keep going
when everything seems difficult
and hopeless.

**From:** trudi trouncer
**Sent:** 21 September 2006 15:22
**To:** jenny gelly
**Subject:** my support group

Hello gang,

My vision
My visions are to climb Mont Blanc and to set up my own
business breeding poodles.

My accomplishments last week
I went to check out a rock climbing school and got all
the info on course dates and fees.
I sent off my application form to register with the UK
poodle breeder's club.
Fingers crossed they approve me.

My actions for this week
I will enroll in the October rock-climbing course.
I will research on the internet various ways to advertise
puppies for sale.

Challenges I now face
I need to be there for my son whilst he's doing his
A-levels.

Opportunities
There is an adventure holiday expo at Olympia next week.
I will be there.
I may discuss business partnership with my aunt who
breeds Labradors. Just need to pick up the phone and
invite her for tea.

What I need
A new internet service provider and once-a-week
babysitter.

What I want
George Clooney to sweep my off my feet. Failing that,
a weekend break in Brighton.

Thanks for your support. Can't wait to see you all at
the next meeting.

T x

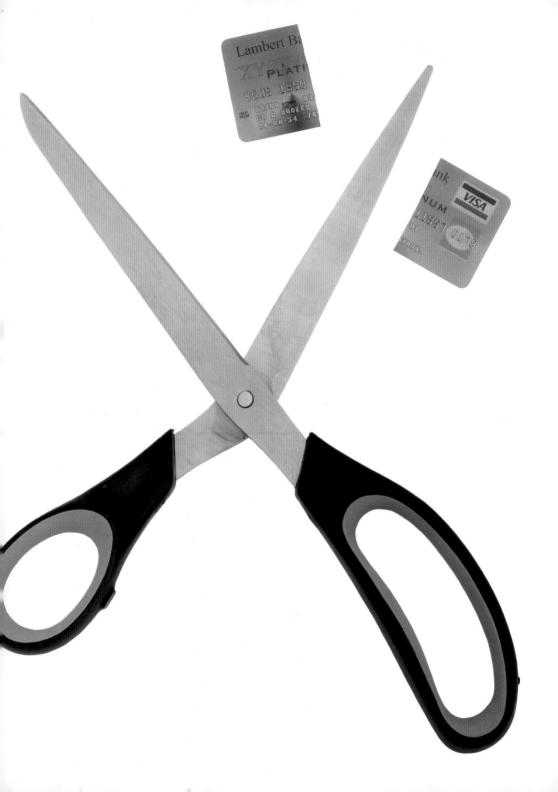

# WHAT WOULD YOU

# GIVE UP?

Two most common excuses for staying stuck are 'I don't have time' and 'I can't afford it'. We all spend a great deal of time and money trying to compensate for something that we feel is lacking in our lives. Aimless shopping and surfing the internet are two strong examples of this, but it can take more subtle, often seemingly justifiable forms. Maybe you go to numerous exercise classes. Ask yourself how fit you really need to be. Or you might be giving excessive amounts of money to charities. Do you do this to help others, or to make yourself feel better?

Go back to your pressure group with your diary and your bank and credit card statements. Lay the facts honestly in front of them. Be prepared to answer the question, 'What would I be prepared to give up in order to get what I truly desire?' It is surprising how others can find time and money in our lives where we thought there was none.

An old Cherokee chief is teaching his grandson about life.

'A terrible fight is going on inside me. The same fight is going on inside you, and inside every other person too. It is a fight between two wolves. The first wolf speaks to me of evil – anger, guilt, shame, envy, resentment, self-pity, dishonesty, self-doubt and ego. The other wolf speaks to me of good – joy, peace, love, serenity, self-confidence, courage, kindness, humility, generosity, truth, compassion and faith.'

Wide-eyed, the young boy thought about this, then asked his grandfather: 'But which wolf will win?'

The old chief simply replied, 'The one I feed.'

 writer writes, every day.
A singer sings, every day.
A chef cooks, every day.

You have a job, kids to feed, friends to see, a husband to fuss over, bills to pay – aaaaargh! If only you could chuck it all in and be a student again.

But would you, really?

# GREAT COURSES FOR A FEW DAYS

Pressures of daily life don't generally allow for the luxury of full-time education. How we sometimes long to just immerse ourselves in learning and practising a pursuit we've always hankered after. An intensive residential course is a great way to kick-start into something new – and find out if it really is for you.

## Writing

The Arvon Foundation runs one-week residential courses in every conceivable form of creative writing at four centres around the UK: www.arvonfoundation.org

Poetry courses around the world are listed at: www.poetrykit.org

For more ideas look at www.writers-circles.com www.writehereinfrance.co.uk www.author-network.com

## Driving skills

Take the stress out of learning to drive. Find an intensive residential course at: www.2pass.co.uk www.learners.co.uk www.crashcourses.net

## Cooking

So many enticing courses to choose from – our eyes might end up being bigger than our bellies.

In the hills of southern Tuscany Il Rigo is one of the original organic farms of the area. Cookery courses concentrate on regional cuisine using seasonal local produce. Specialised topics include bread and pasta making and cooking with saffron. www.ilrigo.com

For more ideas visit: www.tastingplaces.com http://cookforfun.shawguides.com www.italiangourmet.com www.responsibletravel.com www.theinternationalkitchen.com

## Humanities

Bristol University offers a varied programme of residential courses throughout the year. www.bristol.ac.uk

## Outdoor pursuits

Rock climbing worldwide www.rockandsun.com

Scuba diving at home and abroad: www.scuba-dive.co.uk

For a list of outdoor and adventure breaks in the Highlands, visit www.scotland-inverness.co.uk

## Art and crafts

A great guide to art courses for adults and children nationwide. www.artcourses.co.uk

Summer masterclasses are offered at Yorkshire Sculpture Park: www.ysp.co.uk

www.travel-quest.co.uk is a specialist travel directory that lists a variety of inspiring courses in crafts, photography and painting all over the world.

A website dedicated to all crafty things: www.craft-fair.co.uk lists crafts courses, including residential, nationwide.

## Music

Study classical music in a lakeside setting with courses for all abilities. www.jackdaws.org.uk

A summer programme of week-long residential courses at Sherborne School in Dorset is available through www.canfordsummerschool.co.uk

Share Music runs week-long residential courses in performing arts for people with physical disabilities in England, Northern Ireland and Sweden. www.sharemusic.org.uk

Find out about one week and weekend courses in jazz for all levels at www.jazzcourse.co.uk

## Building

Stay in an eco-cabin in Powys and learn about alternative building technologies. www.cat.org.uk

## More information

Hillcroft College in Surrey runs residential courses in life and work skills for women only. www.hillcroft.ac.uk

A huge variety of City and Guilds learning breaks, from palaeography to philosophy to papier mâché, are listed at www.timetolearn.org.uk

University of Cambridge's Institute of Continuing Education runs diverse academic residential courses at beautiful Madingley Hall. No academic qualifications are required. www.cont-ed.cam.ac.uk

# LEARN FROM HOME

**The internet has revolutionised the way the terminally busy can undertake education. Sign on for a distance-learning course and read your lectures, submit your essays or chat to your classmates in Chicago – all at six o'clock in the morning!**

## Writing

New York-based writing school Gotham offers excellent online writing courses, ranging from screenwriting to travel writing and seminars in how to get published.
www.writingclasses.com

www.writingclasses.co.uk runs 10-week online courses in creative writing and poetry.

Birkbeck College offers distance-learning courses in writing, earth sciences, geology and biology.
www.bbk.ac.uk/study/all_courses/subjects/distancelearning

## Free coures

Free computer skills courses are available on the internet at www.homeandlearn.co.uk

American bookstore Barnes & Noble includes lists of free courses and reading groups on their website. Click on the B&N University tab at www.barnesandnoble.com

News University offers free courses in the field of journalism and copywriting.
www.newsu.org

## Other valuable sites

Massachusetts Institute of technology (MIT) offers 'Open Course Ware', a vast resource of materials and assignments that are used in their degree courses. Free online at http://ocw.mit.edu

The world-beating BBC website lists a range of courses too huge to detail, including information about the excellent BBC Learning Zone.
www.bbc.co.uk/learning

The British Council's Education UK website is aimed at overseas visitors but has a great searchable database for finding distance-learning courses.
www.educationuk.org

Learn astrology from home with the Faculty of Astrological Studies: www.astrology.org.uk

Learndirect lists practical online courses in subjects such as computers, office skills, self-development or improving your maths or English.
www.learndirect.co.uk

A listing of graduate and post-graduate courses online can be found at http://jobs.guardian.co.uk

The Open University is the original and best distance learning foundation offering undergraduate and post-graduate degrees.
www.open.ac.uk

## Volunteering

Want hands-on experience working in your own time with people in your local area? Volunteering is a great way to learn new skills, build social networks and feel good about yourself Get loads of ideas and practical information at:
www.volunteering.org.uk
www.volunteerscotland.info
www.volunteering-wales.net
www.volunteering-ni.org
www.volunteeringireland.ie

# WHAT I WOULD LIKE TO DO:

'I've always wanted to learn photography properly. This year I am going to make the time.'

# JACKETS THE RULES

## Big tits

A small lapel narrows down the boob area. One button draws the eye down to the waist.

The detail on the waist distracts from the chest.

Tailored structuring and panelling show off an hourglass figure to best advantage.

## No waist

No buttons allow you to pull in the jacket even tighter to give a nipped-in shape.

A jacket that is very fitted and stretchy really creates a great waist.

A well-placed single button draws the eye to the centre of the waist.

# Big tummy

A wider fit jacket worn over a dress skims the tummy and conceals extra rolls.

Small busy print camouflages a larger stomach.

The big belt tie can be draped over an expanding waistline.

# Saddlebags

A long-line jacket covers the saddlebags.

A very short jacket does not cut into the widest line of the hips.

The ruffle on the jacket brings the eye to the waist and away from the saddlebags.

October

| | | | |
|---|---|---|---|
| 1 | Reassess make-up colours now that your summer glow has faded<br><br>2 | 3 | 4 |
| 9 | 10 | 11 | 12 |
| Plan half term activities<br><br>17 | 18 | 19 | Buy treats for Halloween<br><br>20 |
| 25 | 26 | Organise Bonfire night<br><br>27 | 28 |

OCTOBER

| | | | |
|---|---|---|---|
| | | Clean and store away all your summer clothes | |
| 5 | 6 | 7 | 8 |
| Bleed all your radiators | | | |
| 13 | 14 | 15 | 16 |
| | | | |
| 21 | 22 | 23 | 24 |
| | | | |
| 29 | 30 | 31 | |

'Once a month, wash your engagement ring gently with an old toothbrush and fairy liquid. You will get lots of compliments.'

# Alterations

### Coats
Add a fur or feather collar to an old coat to give it a new lease of life. Double-breasted coats and jackets suit very few women yet we find so many lurking in the backs of wardrobes. Take all your old double-breasted garments and transform them into single breasted. It's a job for a tailor that involves cutting down the front panels and moving the buttons.

### Trousers
Any trousers that are not drainpipes feel luxurious and make legs look longer when they fall to the floor. Have trousers altered so they end just at the bottom of the heel – of your shoe, not your foot. Don't always limit yourself to the petite section if you are short. Just buy that great pair of trousers and have them taken up. It will add £10–15 to the price, but will be worth it if they're the right shape for your leg. If your legs are endless, always check that there is enough hem to let down. Use a tape binding if necessary. Trouser leg shapes come and go. If the shape of some of your trouser legs is looking dated, crop them off below the knee and wear them with long boots.

'I haven't got a thing to wear', we often wail melodramatically. Usually we find that it's not garments that we lack – it's imagination. A bit of planning and inspiration will turn what seem like old rags into new robes.

# CLOTHES
## MAKING NEW FROM OLD

## Bags
Take the tired strap off a favourite handbag and then use the bag as a clutch bag.

## Dresses
If you fall in love with a vintage dress that is too big and too short, have it taken in and use the extra fabric to create the hem length you want.

## Shirts
If you suffer from a long back, most shirts hang wide and badly around your bum. To give yourself the best shape possible have them taken in and a zip put down the side instead.

## Skirts
Now that you know your best skirt lengths (see pages 90-1), have all your skirts adjusted to suit. Taking the waistband off an old skirt and replacing it with a simple ribbon or binding will make it bigger.

## Jumpers
We love cashmere sweaters but the fibre is so delicate that they tend to wear through on the elbows much sooner than our wool sweaters. It seems a shame to waste this luxurious fabric so we turn them into pretty vests that look amazing worn over a floaty shirt in winter. Cut the sleeves off and tidy up the raw edges with an overlocker or by hand with blanket-stitch. Use embroidery to cover stains or holes. Any tiny moth holes on the body can also be decorated with blanket stitching in a complementing colour. You can jazz it up with an embroidered patch on the front or shoulder. Got too many polo necks and crew necks? Slash the jumpers off at the shoulder and finish with some lovely brocade or two-inch velvet ribbon where your bra straps sit to create an evening top.

## Buttons

BUTTONS can be the most dating thing about a jacket. Gold buttons scream 1980s. Replacing the buttons on a jacket can really change its mood. Try filigree buttons on a cinched jacket to give it an authentic 1950s feel or big clear plastic buttons to modernise a coat. Although we are great advocates of High Street clothes they do tend to use cheap buttons. With a simple button face-lift no one will ever guess where you got it.

# STAINS, MOTHS & OTHER NASTIES

## Kill the spill

If we spill a little bit of food on our clothes we try to resist the urge to tear the garment from our bodies and jump in a taxi to go to the nearest dry cleaner. Instead we remember three simple points.

**First** Deal with it immediately. Most substances take time to penetrate fibres so the longer you leave it the worse the stain will be.

**Second** Forget what your grandma told you about white wine and lemons, a wet wipe is the best instant stain remover for all fabrics, except for satin. For spills on satin, use a clean white napkin to absorb the stain, then dampen it with cold water or soda water and gently blot the stain. A little bit of fairy liquid with water is good for greasy food on jumpers.

**Third** Don't apply heat of any kind. It will set the stain. This means, don't use hot water.

## Vigilance and cleaning are the keys to moth control

**Never bring second-hand clothes into your wardrobe without cleaning them first.**
Never put clothes away with sweat or food stains on them.
**Moths are happiest in dark, undisturbed corners. Rotate summer and winter clothes and don't leave old hats, scarves or blankets undisturbed for a long time.**
Vacuum clean the edges of carpets and under the furniture, likewise down the back of the sofa.

## Love your smalls

Put bras, knickers, tights and socks inside a net bag or an old stocking tied up at the top before washing. This will prevent straps or odd socks being sucked into the drainage.

# Keeping moths at bay

Clothes moths are golden in colour and look like tiny darts. Any other kinds of moth will not eat your clothes. It's not the actual moth that causes the damage but their larvae that feed on your fabrics when they hatch. The egg cases are those little cobwebby patches that look like spit. Moth larvae love to eat proteins so they are highly attracted to wool, silk, fur and feathers. Food and sweat stains also ring their dinner bell.

The best way to deal with moths is to prevent them getting a foothold. We always wash or dry clean our clothes before putting them away for the summer. Store them in their plastic wrappers. Mothballs do kill moths if the fumes are in high concentration, so this means storing garments in a box with a well-fitting lid. However, the mothballs make clothes smell awful. The smell of cedar wood has moth-repelling properties, but, again, it needs to be in high concentration. You can buy cedar balls or break up old cigar boxes, which are made of cedar.

If sweaters contain unhatched moth eggs, fold them into ziplock bags and then shove them into the freezer overnight to kill the eggs. Make sure you remember to remove the sweaters in the morning otherwise they might end up in the oven with the Sunday roast.

In an utter crisis, Trinny has used a spray called Doom. It's probably more toxic than a nuclear power station, but it does kill all the moths. Spray it inside the cupboard and then close the doors for a few hours. Always make sure clothes are thoroughly aired before wearing them. Never spray bedding with insecticide.

Feather and down duvets and pillows can be washed once or twice a year to help control dust mites.

- Take them to a laundrette where they have the giant washing machines.
- Use a gentle handwash detergent, such as Woolite
- Dry them at low temperature in the big tumble dryers.
- Make sure they are completely dry before storing otherwise a cupboard full of mildew awaits you.

# MAKING SPACE
## TO BUY MORE

Blocks under bed legs make the bed higher so you can fit clear boxes underneath for more storage space.

Build a small shelf above your hanging rails for extra space for jumpers.

Keep shoes in their boxes and label with a Polaroid on the box so you know what's inside.

Hang necklaces on hooks on the inside of your cupboards.

Put knickers and bras in separate dividers for quick access on a busy morning.

If your shelves have space in between each one, think about buying plastic baskets with arms that hook on – they will give you double the amount of storage space.

Fold jumpers to half their normal size to create space for lower and more manageable piles, and then arrange them by colour.

Buy clear Perspex boxes from Muji to store small items of jewellery so that they can be easily seen.

Hang dainty evening bags on the inside of your cupboards.

Put day bags in clear ziplock freezer bags and stuff with newspaper so they don't loose their shape. Remember bags are worth polishing too.

Only keep the season's clothes in your wardrobe (summer or winter) and fold the rest away. This will give you more space to see what clothes you actually have.

If you have space above your wardrobe for items, make sure you keep them in a large wicker basket, this will keep them tidy and make the room appear bigger.

Hang belts on a rail inside your cupboard door.

Shelves in your hanging cupboard are normally 22 inches deep. This should give you room to double up on your folded clothes piles and put less worn garments at the back of the shelf.

To store cosmetics effectively in your bathroom, invest in some clear drawers divided into face, body and hair, and store under the sink. These will help protect items if there is a leak and allow you to find your favourite conditioner more easily.

If you have a small bedroom with a fireplace, build cupboards on either side that only jut out as much as the chimney breast (thereby maintaining the size of your bedroom). This should be just deep enough to store shoes, bags and folded tops as well as all your partner's DVD and satellite paraphernalia.

**Boots** Ideally boots should have been repaired before you put them away for the summer. If you didn't do this, get them re-heeled and re-soled now. Before we put them away we coat them in polish (and don't rub it off) and store them with wooden boot trees, or we stuff the feet with newspaper and use plastic trees for the legs. The polish feeds and protects the leather through the summer months. When they emerge from hibernation in the autumn, all we have to do is give them a good shine. Always use boot trees. And it's useful to know boot shapers will stop boot legs from developing nasty creases at the ankles.

# BEFORE YOU PUT IT AWAY

**Footwear** Always use shoe trees. Leather shoes that get a lot of wear need untreated wooden shoe trees (these absorb sweat and dampness from the leather; plastic or varnished wooden shoe trees are not absorbent). The little foam half-shapers are great for sandals. If you have a watermark line on a leather shoe, rub it with a cut potato and then polish to remove the mark. Hairspray will take biro marks out of leather items. Cif is great for getting marks off non-leather goods – white trainers, rubber flip-flops and the like can all be cleaned with Cif scouring paste and a toothbrush.

**Hats** Hats can be stored one inside the other (the widest brims at the bottom) in a big hatbox. Be aware that moths can get into felt and fur hats. Straw hats should never be stored above a radiator because they will dry out and become brittle. If a hat gets bent out of shape, reshape it over the steam from a kettle.

**Knitwear** Shave bobbles on knitwear with a sharp razor or a special battery-operated de-bobbling device (available at John Lewis). Avoid combs or implements that pull the fibres. Dry cleaning will make cashmere go hard. Hand wash, then roll inside a towel and press down hard to get out the excess water. Dry flat. Add a capful of vinegar to your final rinse for woollens, it will make them more fluffy.

**Bras** Remember to put bras inside the leg of an old stocking before popping them into the washing machine. Bra underwires are finished with little plastic caps. Don't wash or dry at a high temperature because the caps will melt and the underwires will poke through the fabric of the bra.

Nothing will ruin clothes more quickly than keeping them on those wire hangers from the dry cleaner. Any knitted or jersey garments will develop unsightly 'shoulder-wings' while coats and jackets will become misshapen hunchbacks. Every time a garment crosses our threshold it is immediately transferred onto a fit-for-purpose hanger.

## For knits

Such as jersey, silk, chiffon and all delicates: use padded satin hangers.

## For coats and jackets

Use hangers with wide, shaped shoulders.

## For heavy skirts

Use hangers with padded clips (so there won't be nasty bite marks on your skirts).

## For lightweight skirts

Use hangers with slits for hanging loops.

## For trousers

Use clamp hangers and hang the trousers by their hems (unless they are half-lined in which case they should be hung over the bar of a straight hanger).

## For suits

Use proper suit hangers with padded clips. This might seem like you will need a lot of space, but remember how few of your clothes you actually wear. Having a thorough cull or storing out-of-season clothes will allow the garments you really love a chance to come into their own.

# HANGING & ARRANGING

Cherish all your lovely clothes the same. Whether it came from Prada or Primark it deserves a decent hanger.

# TROUSERS THE RULES

## Big bum

Big pockets break up the expanse of bottom.

A wide waistband will horizontally cut the bum in half.

Wide legs hide where the sagging bum ends.

## Short legs

Elongate the leg with a narrow stripe.

No waistband gives the appearance of trousers going on forever.

If your hems touch the ground it will elongate the leg and hide the high heel you are wearing underneath.

# Big tummy

A deep waistband will act as a corset on the tummy

Flat-fronted trousers are best for minimising the tummy area.

A side fastening is better than a zipper jutting out in front.

# Saddlebags

Cropped trousers with turn-ups draw the eye to the bottom half of the leg.

A bootleg cut will balance out the width of the hips.

Wide leg covers saddlebag and thicker thighs.

November

| | | | |
|---|---|---|---|
| 1 | 2 | Buy yourself a treat today — you're worth it<br><br>3 | 4 |
| 9 | 10 | 11 | 12 |
| 17 | Go on the internet to find a discount ski pass<br><br>18 | 19 | 20 |
| 25 | 26 | 27 | Buy Christmas cards<br><br>28 |

NOVEMBER

| 5 | 6 | 7 | 8 |
|---|---|---|---|
|   | Buy your Christmas party dress |   |   |
| **13** | **14** | **15** | **16** |
|   |   | Order turkey or goose and other Christmas dinner essentials |   |
| **21** | **22** | **23** | **24** |
|   | Send Christmas cards to friends and family abroad |   |   |
| **29** | **30** |   |   |

'Add a capful of vinegar to your final rinse for woollens. It will make them more fluffy.'

# HEALTHY, HAPPY & WISE

## A brilliant cold remedy from South America

There are five ingredients:
Juice of a lemon
A big spoonful of honey
About an inch of grated root ginger
A fat clove of garlic, chopped
And, finally, a sliced hot chilli –
a jalapeno or red chilli will do the trick.

**Put all the ingredients in a teapot or big mug, add hot (not boiling) water and stew for 5 minutes. Strain the potion. Hold your nose, drink it down, then wrap up warm, go to bed and sweat it out.**

## And to relieve a sore throat...

**Here's a recipe from France for relieving sore throats. Chop up an onion, quite finely. Put it in a bowl and sprinkle with sugar. Cover and leave for 2 or 3 hours. Strain and drink the juice.**

## Fending off colds

**Dairy products** encourage our bodies to make mucus. Not helpful in the winter months. Replace those fattening lattes with a nice cup of herbal tea or instant miso soup. Or how about having delicious sliced tomatoes and olive oil on toast instead of cheese and pickle?

**Porridge** is delicious made with water instead of milk. It's not the same creature but it's just as yummy. Add a few sultanas or slices of dried apricot, microwave for three minutes, and then top it off with maple syrup. Muesli tastes great topped with apple juice.

**Cold or flu** – what's the difference? We've noticed that on the whole women get colds while men get 'flu'.

At the first sign of a cold we try to give the virus a knockout punch of vitamin C. This means taking 1000 mg every couple of hours. Don't worry you can't overdose on vitamin C. If you do take too much it will give you slight diarrhoea, so stop. NB: do not give large doses of vitamin C to children.

# NO SNUFFLES

# COMFORTING & NOURISHING
# CHICKEN SOUP

Nothing comforts the ill and promotes feelings of being loved like home-made chicken soup. Here's an easy recipe from our fabulous cheffing friend Skye Gyngell.

It is important that all the ingredients are organic.
1 tablespoon vegetable oil
2 carrots, peeled and finely chopped
2 sticks celery, finely chopped
1 leek, washed and chopped (white part only)
1 thumb root ginger, peeled and very finely chopped
1 clove garlic, finely chopped
1 medium red chilli, seeds removed and finely chopped
2 tablespoons coriander leaves, chopped
juice of half a lemon
2 tablespoons tamari or light soy sauce
1 litre organic chicken stock (preferably home-made)
2 organic chicken breasts
1 cup snow peas, shredded
a handful of bean sprouts

Heat the vegetable oil in a heavy-based saucepan large enough to hold all the ingredients. Add the carrots, celery, leeks, ginger, garlic, chilli and coriander, and sweat over a gentle heat for 10 minutes.

Add the lemon juice and tamari (or soy sauce) and stir. Add the stock and bring to the boil. Drop in the chicken breasts and poach for 10 minutes. Remove the chicken and allow to cool slightly, then shred the meat.

Return the shredded chicken to the soup and drop in the noodles. Blanch the snow peas in boiling water for 30 seconds and refresh immediately under cool water. Add to the pot. Adjust the taste as necessary with a few extra drops of tamari, soy sauce or lemon juice.

Add the bean sprouts just before serving so they stay really crunchy.

# MEDICAL ✚
# MOMENTS AT HOME

We both achieved our Red Cross badges and wore them with pride. Do we remember any of those vital skills now that we have families of our own? Not likely. But we have spoken to our friends at the British Red Cross and here are their suggestions on what to do when faced with common accidents and mishaps around the house.

### Burned yourself on the iron?

**DO** cool the burn by running it under cold water or completely submerging it in iced water for at least 10 minutes, then cover it with a sterile dressing or cling film.

**DON'T** put any lotions and potions on it – or butter like your granny told you!

### Cut your finger while cooking?

**DO** press on the wound with your other hand or a clean cloth. Raise it above the level of your heart and apply a dressing to maintain pressure.

**DON'T** tie the dressing so tightly that it cuts off the circulation.

### Tripped in your heels and twisted your ankle?

**DO** sit down and rest your ankle. Wrap frozen peas in a tea towel and cool the ankle for at least 10 minutes. Bandage the ankle firmly enough to give support and keep it elevated, for example, by resting it on a chair. Remember RICE – Rest, Ice, Compress, Elevate.

**DON'T** try to walk it off.

### Best friend choking on their dinner?

**DO** encourage them to cough. If they can't cough or respond to you, give them up to five back blows with the heel of your hand. Check in the mouth for dislodged food. If this fails, come from behind them and place clenched fists just below the ribs and pull inwards and upwards.

Do this up to five times. Check the mouth again for dislodged objects. Continue with another two cycles of five back blows and five abdominal thrusts. Call an ambulance if they are still choking.

**DON'T** pat them lightly on the back if choking is severe. Back blows should be given with some force.

### Got a nosebleed?

**DO** pinch the soft part of your nose for 10 minutes and tip your head forward. If bleeding continues, pinch the nose again for a further 10 minutes. If it continues for more than 30 minutes, seek medical advice.
**DON'T** tip your head back.

### Chest pains?

You notice your elderly neighbour clutching his chest and in obvious pain. You suspect he's having a heart attack.
**DO** help him to sit down, call an ambulance and get him to chew an aspirin.
**DON'T** let him eat, drink or smoke.

### Too much to drink?

Your teenage son arrives home drunk and you want to put him to sleep in the recovery position to be safe.
**DO** lie him on the floor, turn him on his side, tilt his head back and make sure his airway is open so he can breathe.
**DON'T** put him to bed and leave him lying on his back. Also, don't put anything thick under his head, such as a pillow.

## Your toddler's swallowed detergent?

**DO** wipe his mouth, call for medical help and get him to take frequent sips of cold water or milk.

**DON'T** try to make him vomit – the chemicals may cause more harm on the way back up!

## Pills instead of sweets?

Your daughter has eaten pills from your bathroom cabinet thinking they were sweets.

**DO** try and find out what, when and how much she took. Call an ambulance immediately.

**DON'T** try to make her vomit – the chemicals may cause more harm on the way back up!

## Fallen into water?

You took your eye off your toddler for two minutes and discover he's fallen into the garden pond.

**DO** immediately get him out of the water. If he's not breathing, give him five rescue breaths, then alternate 30 chest compressions with two breaths for one minute before calling an ambulance. If you have help, call an ambulance as soon as you know he's not breathing.

**DON'T** assume he is OK if he has recovered, as he may have inhaled some water.

If in doubt, seek medical advice in any circumstance. Call your GP or NHS Direct (0845 46 47).

The British Red Cross produces a brilliant series of 5 Minute First Aid guides. Every home should have these guides. Visit www.redcross.org.uk/firstaid or call 0870 170 9222.

**For a few women the hormonal change brought on by the onset of periods, and later the menopause, is a breeze. For the majority it is something entirely different. We've consulted the experts for some insight into how to allay the symptoms.**

Leading holistic naturopath Roberta Stimson says:
In general, both premenstrual syndrome and menopausal symptoms are pretty much unheard of in countries where life is simple and there is a balance of fresh home-cooked food, physical exertion, a well-occupied mind and the support of loving family life.

In the West our lives have become overly complicated. The stress levels acquired throughout life affect the endocrine system, in particular the adrenals, eventually creating over- or under-functioning glands.

It is primarily the adrenal glands that give us the strength and courage to get through each day, fending off whatever challenges we're dealt and then waking up the next day ready to start all over again!

The adrenal glands also allow us to cope with change, including the monthly intrusion of a period, or the emotional and physical effects of menopause, the ultimate 'change' for a woman.

# CONQUERING
## PMT & THE MENOPAUSE

The following suggestions will help redress the balance and ease the symptons:

**EAT WELL**
Eat three moderate meals a day, with two small protein snacks such as nuts or a hard-boiled egg in between meals.

**VARY YOUR DIET**
Make sure that each meal contains about 50% protein, 30% vegetables (NOT including potato), and 20% other carbohydrates, including fruit.

**EAT REGULARLY**
Make it a rule never to skip meals even if the 'meal' is a yoghurt smoothie, a few natural raw nuts and seeds, cottage cheese, low-fat hummus or organic peanut butter on a rice cake, some tinned fish, or even a soya protein drink. If we skip meals or have a carb snack in desperation our adrenal glands are put under enormous strain causing a shift in blood-sugar levels which ultimately robs us of precious energy. By the time it's 'that time of the month' or that time of one's life, there isn't the energy needed to handle our natural bodily processes, leaving us prone to mood-swings, including anger, aggression and irritability, over-sensitivity, weepiness, and a feeling of vulnerability.

**AVOID**
Stay away from refined carbohydrates, all wheat products if possible, and salty foods which depress the metabolism, create bloating and water-retention and cause food-allergy symptoms of fuzzy-headedness, constipation, pressure, mood-swings, muscle soreness, weight gain and skin problems!

# Fluctuating energy levels

Diet is key to maintaining energy levels. Those who are conscious of fluctuations in energy levels have been shown to eat a lot of refined carbohydrates, skip meals because they're too busy or on a 'diet', probably drink coffee or copious amounts of tea or soft drinks, and smoke cigarettes. This causes over stimulation of the adrenal glands, and causes vulnerability to natural body changes. Post-natal depression, for example, is related to adrenal exhaustion.

**Here are recommended supplements to a good quality diet:**

Omega-3 fish oil – 1–3 grams daily – for good calcium absorption, heart and cardiovascular strength, brain function, including good memory, concentration and peace of mind, a balanced nervous system, and healthy skin, teeth and bones.

**A top quality, no-expenses-spared multi-vitamin and mineral that contains all the vital minerals, including iron glycinate, magnesium and trace elements, vitamin E and also containing the B-complex group of vitamins – among them B6, at an average dose of 50–100 mg.**

Digestive support in the form of betaine hydrochloride. We produce up to 50% less of this stomach acid from the age of 40, leaving us more susceptible to poor digestion, bacterial or parasitic infection and in particular to bone density reduction due to poor assimilation of calcium and other minerals. Take this with the main meal every day from the age of 30 if there is a family history of osteoporosis, or from 40 onwards in general.

**Most omega-6 oils are easily obtained in the diet. However, one specific type – gamma linolenic acid (GLA) – is not, so take evening primrose or starflower oil at a dose of 2000–4000 mg daily for at least two weeks before periods are due to start. It can also be taken throughout the month.**

Take 1000 mg of time-released vitamin C with evening meals to assist healing of the adrenals during sleep.

**Check with your doctor before taking supplements to ensure they are the right combinations and dosages for you.**

## One of our favourite teas

Mix equal quantities
of green tea, dried rosehips
and dried rose flowers (these must
be edible quality – don't dry your
own roses from the florist as
they will have been drenched
in pesticides), and brew. Dried
rose flowers and rosehips
are available from

www.nealsyardremedies.com

# Other ways to help correct imbalances

### Relaxation
Lie down for 20–30 minutes in the middle of the day with headphones on and a calming hypnotherapy CD. Let thoughts pass through your mind and out the other side. The effect is profound and immediate.

### Chiropractic adjustments
Have them regularly, say four times a year. Keeping the spine flexible allows free circulation around the nerves and blood vessels, which connect like an internal wiring system to all our organs and glands.

### Yoga and pilates
For muscle strength, flexibility, balance and calm, as well as gentle stimulation of glands and organs for optimal function and healthy cycles.

### Colon hydrotherapy
Two or three treatments a year can assist in reducing a build-up of pressure in the gut as a result of hidden constipation, gas or bacterial imbalance, all of which can affect the mind, skin, hormonal balance and digestion in a negative way.

### How to keep your colon clean

A probiotic capsule first thing each morning

½ teaspoon barley grass powder in water, daily

Eat bran regularly

Eat an apple a day

Drink a glass of hot water
with lemon every morning

Eat plenty of vegetables,
particularly steamed broccoli,
with olive oil and garlic

# Period pain

Debilitating period pain and abdominal discomfort is often associated with backache and groin pain. An ice pack placed across the lower back for 10–20 minutes can relieve discomfort tremendously. It may sound like the last thing you'd want to do, but wrap up warm and try it for a great result. With thanks to Roberta Stimson at the Gonstead Clinic www. gonstead.co.uk

### Exercises to stimulate the hormones
Recommended by Dr Nonna Brenner

1 Draw in and squeeze the muscles in the lower abdomen. Repeat three times.

2 Exercise the muscles in the vagina area. Feel like you are going for a pee and then stop. Do this three times.

3 Bend from the waist and as you straighten up, repeat step 1 three times.

4 While sitting down, relax and then tighten the vaginal muscles three times.

5 In the sitting position, feel like the vaginal muscles are pulling something upwards. Repeat three times.

6 While doing the housework or running around the office, cross the knees one in front of the other as you walk in a straight line. At the same time pull the leg muscles up towards the vagina. Do this three times.

7 Lie down on your back with your legs in the air. Put your arms and hand by your sides and use them to lift your bottom and legs at a 45-degree angle into the air for two to three minutes.

8 To massage the liver: sit, place hands below your breastbone. Using four fingers massage the area in sweeping movement across your ribcage from the middle to the sides.

As your stamina improves, build up to 10 repetitions of each exercise.

# 12 exercises to help balance the hormonal system

**Recommended by Dr Nonna Brenner**

Before you start the series of exercises on the opposite page, stand at ease with your hands loosely clenched and then flick them open and closed in the direction of the movement. Imagine you are flicking water from the ends of your fingers.

Breathing correctly is important. Take short, sharp breaths in through the nose and out through the mouth with each movement. Focus on breathing in more than breathing out with each movement, as if you have just caught an unpleasant whiff of manure.

Always do these exercises in sets of eights, building to 16, 24, 32, etc., up to a maximum of 96 each.

# The Exercises

Flick your hands open and closed, extending your arms forwards in front of your chest.

Flick your hands open and closed, extending your arms down towards the floor.

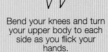

Bend your knees and turn your upper body to each side as you flick your hands.

Pat yourself on the back with both hands, right arm over left.

Pat yourself on the back with both hands, left arm over right.

Pat yourself on the back and then lean forwards with a straight back flicking your arms and hands towards the floor. Alternate arms with each patting on the back.

Keep your head erect and rotate it from side to side with each sharp breath.

Move your head from shoulder to shoulder with each breath.

Move your head forwards and back with each breath.

Lunge forwards while flicking arms and hands towards the floor.

Lift knees up and down alternately (as if marching on the spot) while flicking arms and hands down by your sides.

Kick your back legs alternately towards your bottom while flicking arms and hands down towards the floor.

# COATS THE RULES

## Big tits

The slanted pockets and flared skirt
complement the hourglass shape.

The band just below the breasts
emphasises the slimmest part of the body
and gives a narrower silhouette.

## No waist

The tie belt can be winched to give
the appearance of a smaller waist.

The plunging V neckline draws
the eye to the centre of the waist.

# Big shoulders

The wide lapel breaks the
width of the shoulders.

The longer the coat, the
narrower the shoulders.

# Saddlebags

A knee-length spring coat completely
covers saddlebags. It can be worn as a
jacket and not taken off.

A Nehru collar makes the
shoulders seem broader, thus
balancing the width of the hips.

12

December

| | | | |
|---|---|---|---|
| Order your Christmas tree | Write Christmas card lists | | |
| **1** | **2** | **3** | **4** |
| | | | Send Christmas cards |
| **9** | **10** | **11** | **12** |
| Check you've bought all the presents — and a few spares | | | |
| **17** | **18** | **19** | **20** |
| | | | Write a list of everyone who sent you a Christmas card and add it to your Christmas card list |
| **25** | **26** | **27** | **28** |

DECEMBER

| 5 | 6 | 7 | 8 |
|---|---|---|---|
| | Make sure you are well stocked with all the basics | | Check that your fairy lights are working |
| 13 | 14 | 15 | 16 |
| Make lists of fruit, veg and other fresh foods | | | |
| 21 | 22 | 23 | 24 |
| | | | |
| 29 | 30 | 31 | |

'If you have to give gifts to lots of children, take your budget to the local toy shop and ask for their recommendations. They know the latest thing better than anyone.'

Why is giving and buying presents such a stressful business?

Is it because we want to get it right? Is it because we want a positive reaction? Or is it because the gift is a reflection on us and a representation of what we feel about the person we are giving it to? Be honest, it's not just the thought that counts. The fact is we are disappointed when we give or receive something inappropriate. We say things like, 'Oh it's just something silly' and 'You can change it if you don't like it' to hide our nervousness of getting it wrong and pre-empt the possibility that your friend/lover/boss/dad might hate what you have bestowed so generously.

All this anxiety makes finding our offering extremely fraught. We can't shop for you, but we can help in working out what gift will be a success.

The answer to great giving lies both in the gift and the person you are giving to. Example: a bunch of bluebells means zilch to your boss but everything to the friend who patched your grazed knee after you cut it falling in a bluebell wood. By the same token, a powerful businessman who has gained success through control is hardly going to appreciate a cuddly toy rabbit, but he will appreciate the vibrating kind if he is master of it and therefore his wife's or mistress's pleasure.

We have found working with someone's motivations is an almost foolproof route to successful gift giving. If you work out what makes the person tick and what motivates them, the odds on making their day with your present become very good.

When it comes to a person's purpose in life it seems that there are three clear types. You may find that in adapting these to your friends and loved ones there are those who fit into two of the categories on the following pages. That's fine. There will never, however, be someone who fits in to all three.

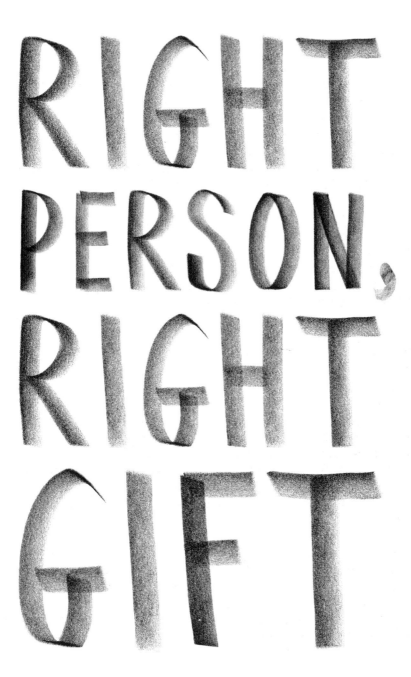

RIGHT PERSON, RIGHT GIFT

# the leader

The Leader who is driven by a need to control. These are normally very successful people. Traditionally they feel a little uncomfortable being given to. They would much rather be the generous one and usually they are …tremendously so. They love gadgets or things that help them control their environment.

## Leader's characteristics to look out for

**Intelligent**
**Dominant**
**Decisive**
**Leadership**
**Arrogant**
**Confident**
**Unemotional**
**Money driven**
**Forceful**
**Influential**
**Inspirational**

## Famous Leaders

**Alan Sugar**
**Philip Green (also a Go Getter)**
**Margaret Thatcher**
**Madonna**
**Elton John (also a big Softie)**
**Jamie Oliver (also a Softie)**
**Angelina Jolie**
**Trinny Woodall (also a Go Getter)**

## Gifts for Leaders

**A stylish business card holder**
**A customised steering wheel**
**A set of free weights**
**Monogrammed luggage**
**A hand-held, all-in-one electronic personal organiser, communications centre and fly-swatter**
**Dinner at home – cooked by a professional chef**

# the go getter

The Go Getter wants to achieve or be perceived to have made it. These people love a label or something that will help them reach their goal.

## Go Getting characteristics to look out for

Active
Determined
Ambitious
Competitive
Hard working
Winner mentality
Likes flattery
Self-conscious
Confident
Wants to have the best
Wants respect

## Famous Go Getters

Victoria Beckham (and most
Footballers' Wives)
Paris Hilton
Arnold Schwarzenegger
Elizabeth Taylor
Rod Stewart
Guy Ritchie

## Gifts for Go Getters

Personalised
notepaper
Tickets to a concert
(preferably VIP
tickets)
A designer handbag
A day at a top spa or gym
A dedication on the radio
Dinner at an impossible-
to-book restaurant

# the Softie

The Softie wants to love and be loved. The most sensitive of the three will really appreciate a beautifully wrapped gift that shows how much you care for them and value their friendship. It is with these guys that the thought really counts.

## Softie characteristics to look out for

Needs to be liked
Wants to please
Friendly
Caring
Sympathetic
Likes to join in
Indecisive
Doesn't make waves
Needs to belong
Wants approval
Looks after friends
Sociable
Insecure

## Famous Softies

Tara Palmer Tompkinson
Robbie Williams
David Furnish (also a Go Getter)
The Princess of Wales (also a Leader)
Brad Pitt
Susannah Constantine (also a Leader)

## Gifts for Softies

A lottery ticket
A specially inscribed poem (even better
if you wrote it yourself)
Divine chocolates
A locket with your photo in it
A compilation of your favourite music
A home-prepared picnic

# Building a gift drawer

This kind of goes against the grain of bespoke gift giving, but there are times when a random present is needed at short notice. This is especially relevant to children... perhaps not your own but certainly your children's friends or your nephews, nieces and godchildren and their seemingly never-ending stream of birthday parties.

Try to stock up on different gifts that will suit all your various friends – the Leaders, the Go Getters and the Softies.

Creating a dedicated drawer will act as an incentive for you to think ahead and look out for great gifts in your travels.

Keep a supply of gift tags, cards, Sellotape and paper in your gift drawer.

To avoid the shame of returning a gift to the original giver, keep a list of who has given you what in your gift drawer.

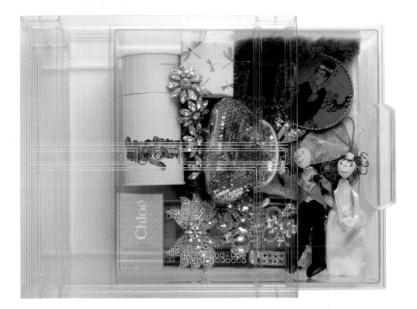

# Feeling skint

**Sometimes the best presents really do cost nothing.**

A voucher offering your services to wash the car or clean the kitchen will bring great delight to the receiver.

Plant a planter with Happy Birthday written in mustard cress seeds a few days beforehand so that they're sprouting nicely on the day.

Cook a delicious meal and do the washing up.

For someone's, say, 40th birthday, write in a card 40 reasons why they're special.

A lottery ticket keeps hope alive.

For a housewarming present, research the local area, find out the best takeaways, local doctor, public transport information, rubbish collection days etc. Give this stress-relieving info pack tied up with a huge ribbon.

Plant a window box and leave it on their windowsill for when they come home.

If you have known someone for a long time, there's nothing more heart warming than giving a copy of an old photograph of them, or a photocopy of an old letter that they sent you long ago.

Keep your parents in touch with your life by chronicling your year in an album that contains photos, thoughts and mementos of your life. No one else will be interested, but mum and dad will love this.

A copy of a newspaper from the day of someone's birth is always an inexpensive winner.

For a recently single friend, write down all your favourite easy recipes and present it in a plastic folder. Better still, fill their freezer with portions of your own home-cooked casseroles in Tupperware boxes.

Anything that you have made yourself will be treasured. The time you spent making it speaks volumes about how much you care.

# GREAT GIFT IDEAS

There are unexpected occasions that pop up through the year that necessitate a well-chosen gift – christenings, dinner parties, romantic moments (including your anniversary)...and what do you get for that tricky customer who has everything? Here are some great ideas.

## Anniversaries

1   **PAPER** good quality personalised stationery.

2   **COTTON** a baby pillow with a favourite saying embroidered on the front.

3   **LEATHER** a leather-bound, blank-paged book with the year and your loved one's name embossed on the front.

4   **LINEN** a linen hankie for every day of the week, each embroidered with a special message.

5   **WOOD** plant five trees. Start an orchard in the country or plant street trees in town (your local council will advise on this).

6   **IRON** a golf club (or a whole set if you're feeling flush).

7   **WOOL** buy a goat for a family in a developing country (many charities offer this service).

8   **BRONZE** have something you treasure (your bust) cast in bronze.

9   **POTTERY** a teacup with a favourite saying painted on it (make your own at a pottery painting shop).

10  **TIN** a first edition Tin-Tin book.

**15 CRYSTAL** a wonderful large crystal in your partner's birthstone.

**20 CHINA** a holiday in China.

**25 SILVER** a silver box. Inside is a note with 25 handwritten reasons why I love you.

**30 PEARL** a dozen oysters – in Paris, in New York or in your local fish restaurant.

**35 CORAL** a diving expedition or holiday on a tropical island.

From here on in, it's precious stones and metals all the way, but please consider – does your partner really want another ring or pair of cufflinks? If jewellery is given, think about how to make it a significant keepsake. One idea, for a golden anniversary, is to have a bracelet or cufflinks engraved with the names and birthdates of all the grandchildren. Or maybe have your partner's name spelled out in tiny diamond chips? It could be much more rewarding to indulge in some great travel. How about a curry – in Bombay – for your ruby anniversary? Or a trip to Ireland for the emerald year? Be creative and spontaneous.

**40 RUBY**

**45 SAPPHIRE**

**50 GOLD**

**55 EMERALD**

**60 DIAMOND**

**75 DOUBLE DIAMOND**

# Christening

**Ideal gifts for babies are things that grow. Build up the following by giving a few pieces each year:**

**A silver cutlery set**

**A china service**

**One pearl at a time to make a necklace**

**One gemstone**

**A charm bracelet**

✳ **Start a collection** that is added to each year.

✳ **Pigs** are always popular to collect, but first-edition books could turn out to be a real winner, too.

✳ **Build a wine cellar** by giving a bottle of wine from each year of their life.

✳ **Plant a tree,** either in the family garden or in a forest

✳ **Adopt an animal** at the zoo.

✳ **Create a time capsule** from the year they were born, to be opened when they are eighteen.

✳ **Start a library** of classic books. This creates a foundation for reading each year, right through to adulthood. We have chosen our favourite titles for little kids and big kids.

✳ **The parents** need a gift, too – engrave a photo frame with the name of their baby.

# Classic books for children and teenagers

**UP TO 1** Ha Ha Maisy by Lucy Cousins. Kipper by Mick Inkpen. **2** Pants by Giles Andreae and Nick Sharratt. Guess How Much I Love You by Sam McBratney and Anita Jeram. **3** Thomas the Tank Engine by W Awdry. Babar by Laurent de Brunhoff. **4** Winnie the Pooh by A A Milne. A Year Full of Stories by Georgie Adams and Selina Young. **5** The Cat in the Hat by Dr Seuss. A Bear Called Paddington by Michael Bond. **6** Horrid Henry's Nits by Francesca Simon and Tony Ross. The Three Little Witches Storybook by Georgie Adams and Emily Bolam. **7** The Worst Witch by Jill Murphy. The Chronicles of Narnia by C S Lewis. **8** Alice in Wonderland by Lewis Carroll. Ballet Shoes by Noel Streatfeild. **9** Wind in the Willows by Kenneth Grahame. Arthur trilogy by Kevin Crossley-Holland. **10** Wolf Brother by Michelle Paver. The Roman Mysteries series by Caroline Lawrence. **11** Shadow of the Minotaur by Alan Gibbons. The Little Prince by Antoine de Saint-Exupery. **12** Lord of the Rings by J R Tolkien. Watership Down by Richard Adams. **13** The Scarecrows by Robert Westall. Harry Potter series by J K Rowling. **14** Sophie's World by Jostein Gaarder. Little Women by Louisa May Alcott. **15** Junk by Melvin Burgess. Astérix by Albert Uderzo and René Goscinny. **16** Catcher in the Rye by J D Salinger. Wuthering Heights by Emily Bronte. **17** Rebecca by Daphne Du Maurier. The Curious Incident of the Dog in the Night-Time by Mark Haddon. **18** Fat is a Feminist Issue by Susie Orbach. Beloved by Toni Morrison.

# Thank you

### For weekends:

People who have guests to stay regularly never have enough hangers. Bring a big pack of quality padded and wooden coat hangers.

A whole ham or a side of smoked salmon is a perfect contribution to the weekend's feeding frenzy.

Great games are always appreciated and everyone can enjoy them.

Bring a box of dressing up stuff – a few wigs and gowns will have everyone in hysterics for hours.

Bring a gift for your friends' beloved pet.

Polaroids or digital photos taken during the weekend should be sent with a thank-you card.

### For a dinner party:

Send flowers to arrive before your hosts' dinner party.

Bring something to enhance the meal, like top quality olive oil.

Fairy lights are a great gift to bring. They instantly transform a room or garden.

Interesting herb teas can be sampled by everybody.

# Gifts that say I love you

Save a memento from somewhere you've been together – a bottle of sand from the beach, a leaf, a dried flower. Give it later as a reminder of a special shared memory.

Use the power of anti-climax. Wrap up an old sock inside which is hidden a note saying 'my other half is under the bed'. There your loved one will find another old sock with a lovely gift inside.

A message spelt out one letter at a time. Leave a chocolate letter or a letter torn from a newspaper headline somewhere that it will be found. Build up your special message over the course of a few days.

Freeze a tiny gift inside an ice-cube and drop it into your lover's drink.

Buy a souvenir of each place that you travel to. Write a message saying 'I love you in Paris', 'I love you in Amsterdam' or 'I love you in Berlin' and send it home.

After a row – flutter a single rose petal through the letter box every day for a week, and ultimately the bare stem with a note 'this is how I feel without you'.

Send a bottle of champagne with two glasses and a note saying 'I'll be round later'.

Cover the bedroom floor with a carpet of rose petals.

You say you will always love each other. Invest in a pendant engraved with appropriate wording, then have it cut in half by a jeweller so that you each wear your part. When the halves are put together the promise will be complete.

As a parting gift – a photo puzzle with one piece missing. The last piece is inserted when you are reunited.

# For the person who has everything

Personalise a T-shirt with one of your in jokes or secret catchphrases.

Have a jigsaw puzzle made from an old photo of your friend.

Name a rose after your friend. This is quite complicated and can take years – so it really shows devotion. The Royal National Rose Society www.rnrs.org is the official body.

A specialist orchid breeder can be commissioned to develop a unique new hybrid of orchid to bear your friend's name and also encourage them to fill their house with blooms.

Name a star after your friend. The unofficial name won't be used by astronomers, but it will show your friend they are sky high in your estimation.

If you've known a successful person before they made it, you probably have incriminating evidence of their past capers. Present them with a beautiful box, or even a decorated shoe box, full of the shredded evidence. Eternal gratitude will be yours.

Make your friend a great mix of all your favourite tunes and load it onto her iPod.

Do what you're good at – and raise money for your friend's favourite charity.

It is possible to lease a row of vines at a vineyard in France and then receive the resulting wine.

Give something fab for their pet – how about a customised dog collar?

If you spend a bit of time together, immortalise it in a photo album for your friend.

Send over a goldfish and a bowl by courier.

**Your friend
has all the latest gadgets
and a wardrobe stuffed with
designer clothes. This person
is a really tricky customer when
it comes to choosing a gift. The
trick is to keep it personal.
Immortalise memories of your
friend and your friendship
and you will be sure
to win their heart.**

# EVENING DRESSES THE RULES

## Big tits

Strapless dress with good support lifts boobs up and out, reducing the look of the whole bust area.

Under 40s can get away with a plunging deep V which halves the chest. Wear a bra with a clear strap across the middle.

## No tits

The extra detail on the chest enhances what little there is.

Tight fitted bodice is a perfect shape for stuffing with chicken fillets to exaggerate the cleavage.

## Big tummy

The weight of the sequins will drag down and flatten any flab.

Front tie detail divides the tummy area.

# Big bum

If you don't have a big tummy, show off your derriere in a dress that hugs under the bum.

Choose a long dress with a flared hem to balance out the expanse of bum.

# Big arms

A loose sleeve in a jersey fabric will drape and not cling over the larger arm.

A small pattern will camouflage the true size of an arm better than a block colour.

# Big hips

Use a gilet in faux fur to widen your shoulders and balance out your hips.

An A-line dress will cover your hips and the sheer chiffon won't add any extra bulk.

our fabulou

# internet directory

# a guide to googling

Knowing how to search most effectively for the information you need is the difference between enjoying the internet and tearing your hair out.

## A few simple terms to understand
A web browser is the software you use to look at the World Wide Web. It could be Internet Explorer, Netscape, Safari or one of many others

A search engine is a service that helps you to find things on the web. The ones we use most often are Google and Ask Jeeves (see opposite), but there are many others such as Alta Vista, the choice of the serious web searcher.

Webmail is mail that you receive on the web. You have to go to a website, such as Hotmail, Excite or Yahoo to look at it. It is not delivered to your computer like email.

## Searching
Obviously you type what you are looking for into the search bar on your search engine. It helps if you know how to spell it correctly, although if you're using Google it will take a guess at it for you. The problem with computers is that they can't read your mind so you have to tell them exactly what you want.

Say, for example, you are looking for a painting holiday and you type in **painting in tuscany**. Your search engine will find every website that contains those three words, although not necessarily in that order.

Using double quotation marks, thus **"painting in tuscany"**, ensures that only the exact phrase you are looking for is found.

But there's still an awful lot to look at, so think about what it is you're really looking for. Is it a landscape painting course? Clever use of the plus sign will narrow your search, so try **"painting in tuscany" +landscape +course.**

You're still finding a lot of unwanted websites offering painting in watercolour courses whereas you want to paint in oils. So use the minus sign to remove the offending term from your results, thus **"painting in tuscany" +landscape +course -watercolour.**

Google's 'Advanced Search' function allows for really precise searching in a number of ways, including by language and by type of website.

## Bookmarks

It's so easy to get sidetracked while surfing. You're happily searching for your painting holiday when a landscape gardening school catches your eye... and you're off into cyberspace. This is what bookmarks are for. Simply click the bookmarks menu on your web browser and add the interesting site. You can visit it later after you've completed your current mission. It's a bit like sticking a post-it note in the Argos catalogue.


## History

After hours of searching you found the ultimate painting holiday, but then the telephone rang and while your back was turned your son got on the internet and now you'll never find your site again! Don't despair, every site you've visited is stored in the history file on your web browser. Just trace your way back through the history list. You will soon find that precious information, and have a peek at what your son has been looking at along the way.


## How to get the best from your search engine

Google is great for finding most things – if you know how to tell it what to find. Sometimes it can be a little difficult. We want to know when Ramadan is so that we can be aware that Muslim friends are fasting and we don't keep rudely inviting them to lunch. Typing **"when is ramadan in 2007"** into Google produces no result because it will only search for that exact phrase. Ask Jeeves, on the other hand, is designed to answer questions. So we typed in **when is ramadan in 2007** (without the quotation marks) and got the answer straight away – as well as lots of other useful information.

We looked up **"trinny and susannah"** on Google and they sound quite interesting. With all their chat about clothes and style, we want to see what they actually look like. So we click on the **'images'** tab just above the Google search bar and bingo – 500 pictures of us!

# buying and selling on the internet

We want to believe in the dream of an internet-enabled, easy-living world, with the promise of effortless shopping at the touch of a button. Goods arrive at our door as if by magic. Instead of queueing at the checkout we're reclining at the manicurist's. If only...

## Safety first
A business on the internet can be based anywhere in the world. It might look like a British company but if it's not actually in the UK it will not be subject to UK consumer protection laws. Ask yourself how much you know about the company before you give them your money. How did you hear about them? Was it a recommendation in a trustworthy magazine, did a friend buy something from them or did you just stumble upon them while surfing the internet? Do they have a verifiable UK address and phone number? For the sake of your sanity and financial security, give a wide berth to retailers who are not contactable by telephone.

Use a separate credit card when buying online. Make sure that the card offers a reasonable level of protection against internet fraud.

Better still, use a pre-paid cash card. You simply charge it up with money and then use it. It's impossible to overspend wildly in a moment of insanity. You can only spend the amount that's on the card. There is a charge per transaction, but no interest to pay. Obviously, this is great if you have teenagers – you'll never have to lend them your credit card again.

Pre-paid cash cards: SNAP: www.snapcard.com; 360 Money: www.360money.com

Never use your debit card on the internet or over the telephone.

## Deliveries
While the internet itself is charging forwards into the future, many retailers' business systems are firmly stuck in the past. The most frustrating aspect of buying online is actually getting your stuff. Ask if you can have a guaranteed delivery slot. The most customer-oriented businesses offer delivery within a two-hour window. If you work in an office, you may consider having your package delivered there during working hours – and then lugging it home on the bus. That still leaves the rest of us – freelancers, mums with kids to collect from school, workers in shops and restaurants, train drivers and so on. Ask the retailer if they deliver during hours that would suit you, like evenings or weekends. If they don't, you really must consider – can I afford to take a whole day

off from my work and life to wait in for that cardigan, or would I be better off popping to the shops on Saturday?

Check your order carefully. One friend of ours was astounded when 74 packs of lamb chops were delivered to his door – and charged to his credit card.


## Returns
Buying an item in cyberspace means that you can't touch it, smell it, try it on or get the feel of it.The dress might be your size, but will it suit your body shape? Always check that the retailer you are dealing with has a no-quibbles returns policy – at their expense, not yours.


## Scams
Phishing is a way of trying to con you into giving out sensitive personal details. An email arrives and it appears to be from your bank. It bears their logo and asks you to go to their website to update your account details because there has been a security breach/software upgrade/data corruption incident. The website looks like your bank's, but once your PIN and account details are entered you'll find your coffers emptied quicker than you can blink. There is only one rule to remember: genuine financial institutions never ask for your PIN or password, either in emails or over the phone. Never give your pin or account details to anyone, no matter how genuine they seem.


## eBay.co.uk
eBay has grown wildly to become the world's most popular place to buy and sell just about anything. Or do we mean "the world's most popular hangout for con-artists and rip-off merchants?" Well, there are problems but eBay's self-regulating system – whereby buyers and sellers rate one another's honesty and efficiency – works surprisingly well. Read eBay's safety tips before you buy or sell. Use your common sense, just as you would when buying from an ad in the local paper or at a street market and you should be fine.


## Buying on eBay
It's relatively easy. You will have to register and jump through all the usual hoops of inventing a username and password (tip: don't use your real name or your mother's maiden name). Use the search bar to find a list of the items you want – the advanced search information page will show you how to refine the list.

Read the description carefully and check the seller's credentials by reading past feedback from other buyers. Check the postage costs (a plastic necklace for £1 ceases to be a bargain if there is a £10 postage charge attached to the price). Make sure that you have the means to pay – is payment requested by cheque, cash or Pay Pal? If you have any questions, email the seller before you bid. **Make sure that the person you are emailing is the same person as the listed seller.**

eBay is an auction, so you bid against other interested buyers. Bidding is likely to be quite stagnant for a while and then go up very quickly towards the end of the auction. Be very clear in your own mind about what your spending limit is so you don't get caught up in the frenzy of the moment and overbid wildly. It is a mistake to bid on several similar items in the hope of winning one of them. You could end up committed to buying four or five things that you don't want.

If you're not sure that you want to bid on an item yet, but you just want to keep an eye on how it's going, you can track it using the 'My eBay' facility. This is a great way to watch several things at once. eBay will email to remind you when each auction is coming to an end, in case you decide to bid at the last minute.

Never get involved with people who contact you directly and try to arrange a deal 'off-eBay' or ask you to pay by Western Union or any other type of untraceable money transfer.

### Selling on eBay

First you'll need to open a seller's account. Just click on the 'sell' button on eBay and follow the step-by-step instructions. You will need to enter your credit card and bank details, so that eBay can check that you're legit and also collect payment for all their charges. eBay makes its money by taking a percentage on each sale, plus various small 'listings charges' for things like adding photographs or giving extra prominence to your item.

Before listing your item it is a good idea to research what similar lots have sold for. You can do a completed listings search by entering a description of your item in the advanced search page and then ticking the box marked completed listings only.

Think carefully about setting a reserve. It's not such a good idea unless you are selling an expensive item such as a car or a watch. Setting a high reserve will only discourage people from getting the bidding started. An auction with 'no bids' can seem off-putting to buyers.

You'll need a digital camera. If you're selling clothes it's a good idea to photograph them on a mannequin. Without being dishonest, try to get a photograph that shows your item at its best. A skirt that's nicely ironed is more likely to sell than one that looks like a crumpled-up dishrag. Also photograph a close-up of the label if it is a designer item. It is important to show any damage or flaws. People are happy to buy if they know exactly what they're getting, but will give you negative feedback if they feel they've been mislead. If your skirt has a broken zip or missing button, photograph a close-up of that area. Make sure that your written description is a fair and detailed reflection of what you're selling.

If you're selling a few things it might be worth opening a Pay Pal account. There are charges, but buyers feel safer using a traceable payment method and this will encourage them to buy from you.

Think about the charge you will make for postage and packaging. How much will it really cost you? Make sure that you package your item properly so that it arrives at its new home undamaged.

Once the auction ends you are obliged to send your item to the highest bidder, as soon as they have sent you the payment. You can't suddenly decide that it has been your favourite skirt for the past ten years and you can't possibly now be parted from it.

If you're too busy or just plain too technophobic to go through the selling process yourself, there are now services that will do it all for you. Auctioning4u will value, photograph and handle your sale, in return for a third of the money! Go to www.auctioning4u.co.uk

After completing any transaction, whether buying or selling, please leave feedback about the person you traded with. Feedback is what keeps the eBay world spinning.

## Spoofs

eBay and Pay Pal attract more than their fair share of fraudsters. Some sell dodgy or non-existent goods, others send very plausible phishing emails. They may ask you to enter your password and details, because they've gone astray, or threaten to report you for not replying to their emails. Never click on links in suspicious emails. If you are unsure about any email purporting to be from eBay or Pay Pal, simply forward it straight away to spoof@ebay.co.uk or spoof@paypal.com.

# beauty

## Beauty products

**www.spacenk.co.uk**
Good: best products online. Beauty at your fingertips.
If you are not sure about which products to use you can get an online consultation.
Bad: nothing.

**www.blissworld.com**
Good: gorgeous site – the graphics make you want to be pampered! Bliss products are truly fabulous.
Bad: to find the UK site you'll need a magnifying glass (it is written in tiny letters at the very bottom of the home page).

**www.myvanitycase.com**
Good: lovely design. Loads of yummy products, from candles to skincare.
Bad: a bit confusing at first.

**www.origins.co.uk**
Good: great layout with a fresh feel, free goodies with your order.
Bad: you will get obsessed and want to buy loads of products. Free delivery over £50.00.

**www.lizearle.com**
Good: each month they feature a special product offer. Very clean

site. A fantastic section on how to shop on their site for first-time internet buyers.
Bad: not much – this is a really great website.

**www.nealsyardremedies.com**
Good: gorgeous natural remedies and you can make your own cosmetics from various ingredients.
Bad: endless chains of slide-out menus make surfing slightly irritating.

**www.jomalone.co.uk**
Good: it's so exciting to be able to buy all Jo Malone's divine products online. The 'gift' section chooses presents for you.
Bad: website could be slicker.

**www.gentlebodycare.co.uk**
Good: natural products for your skin (they do not test on animals) with free delivery in the UK.
Bad: slight supermarket feel to the site.

**www.kornerskincare.com**
Good: slick site packed with deliciously enticing products.
Bad: to you have to download an order form and fax it through.

**www.beautyexpert.co.uk**
Good: no need to pop down to the pharmacy – you can order all your favourite products from here. They also send you free samples with your order.
Bad: so many products that you may end up with hundreds of things you don't need.

**www.renskincare.com**
Good: such a sweet design. These products are to die for – the neroli and grapefruit body wash is one of the best smells you will ever experience.
Bad: nothing, thumbs up all round.

**www.harleycosmetic.com**
Good: buy Jan Marini products from this site (they are amazing for sensitive and problem skins, such as acne).
Bad: a bit confusing at first because there is no introduction to what is available on the site. If you want info on the product you must email first.

**www.drhauschka.co.uk**
Good: what a fab site! You can have an online consultation too.
Bad: not much, this is a great site.

**www.hqhair.com**
Good: the mother site for hair and beauty! Most top make-up artists and hairdressers recommend this site. Very easy to use. Save some money with the online outlet store.
Bad: nothing, this site is fabulous.

**www.beauty-republic.com**
Good: products from all over the world. There is a really great feel about this site and they have put lots of thought into their products. Treat yourself to the pomegranate bath soak. Good links to other natural product sites.
Bad: nothing springs to mind.

**www.elemis.com**
Good: great products.
Bad: the site is somewhat dull and uninspiring.

**www.mybeautyshop.co.uk**
Good: designer make-up at crazy discount prices.
Bad: the site looks cheap and nasty, but it's well worth a visit.

**www.benefitcosmetics.co.uk**
Good: glorious products!
Bad: the homepage isn't great and the 'shop online' link is not very clear and goes through the US.

**www.screenface.com**
Good: professional make-up you can't get anywhere else.
Bad: a basic site, but does the job.

**www.slendertone.co.uk**
Good: we all entertain the dream that we can one day get fit without the bother of diet or exercising. Now we can buy a Slendertone machine without even walking to the shop.
Bad: you still have to diet and exercise.

**www.flowersense.co.uk**
Good: amazing range of flower essences, great description of each potion.
Bad: the site looks very tacky at first, but persevere, it's well worth it!

**www.sttropeztan.com**
Good: buy all the St Tropez products online. Gives clear instructions on how to apply the product at home.
Bad: the before and after photos show a busty blonde with a fabulous body looking pale – and then looking brown!

**www.toniandguy.com**
Good: the gallery section shows hairstyles from chic to crazy. Great for ideas.
Bad: the style that captures your imagination might not actually suit you. Best to ask your stylist for their opinion before insisting on that baroque bird's nest.

## Clinics

**www.thejoshiclinic.com**
Good: this is a super popular top clinic frequented by celebrities. An holistic approach to life.
Bad: too many celebrities!

**www.haleclinic.co.uk**
Good: the mecca for complementary medicine. Very informative and to the point, and you can contact the clinic via email. The ailments list is well worth a look.
Bad: nothing, this is pure information.

**www.lpsa.co.uk**
**www.londonplasticsurgeryasso-ciates.co.uk**
Good: full of useful information about cosmetic surgery. Will answer lots of basic questions about different procedures.
Bad: you can't actually have the surgery done online.

## Spas

**www.islandoutpost.com/spas**
Good: shows tempting spas at funky resort group in Jamaica and the Bahamas.
Bad: will make you acutely aware that you're sitting on your sofa in your pyjamas and it's raining outside.

**www.peraquum.com**
Good: top spas in the Maldives.
Bad: no photos of the actual spas.

**www.palazzoversace.com**
Good: this hotel and spa on Queensland's Gold Coast is as fabulously over the top as we would expect from Donatella Versace.
Bad: More like a city of glitz than a simple, quiet retreat.

**www.hotel-laresidencia.com**
Good: stylish yet simple hotel in the hills of Mallorca. Spa has some great packages like 'bride to be' and 'jet lag eliminator'.
Bad: website design is dead boring.

**www.nuxe.com**
Good: an elegant spa in Paris with some gorgeous treatments.
Bad: it's in Paris.

**www.elemis.com**
Good: top spa in central London.
Bad: tedious website.

**www.lasventanas.com**
Good: beautiful spa in Mexico.
Bad: website is clunky.

**www.chivasom.com**
Good: most spas are just hotels with treatment rooms attached. Chiva Som is a complete holistic health resort with luxury accommodation attached.
Bad: you can't just move in and live there forever.

**www.cowshedclarendoncross.com**
Good: fab website, yummy products, great spa with a café attached! What more do you want?
Bad: it's a bit like being in an episode of 'Sex and The City'.

**www.oneandonlyresorts.com**
Good: super chic spas at jaw-droppingly stylish and expensive resorts around the world.
Bad: slow and complicated website.

# children

## Entertainment

**www.twizzle.co.uk**
Good: for the most magical and imaginative parties.
Bad: expensive!

## Party planners

**www.raspberryproductions.co.uk**
Good: such a genius site! The music might drive you mad after a while. They even organise mini New Year's Eve parties on here.
Bad: rather expensive.

**www.kids-party.com**
Good: everything your area can provide for children: venues, cinema, entertainers, very informative site; covers the whole of the UK.
Bad: not much, great service.

**www.thebluekangaroo.co.uk**
Good: you leave it all up to them! Really takes the stress out of it.
Bad: only available in London.

## Party bags

**www.starbags.info**
Good: these are the most imaginative party bags around.
Bad: you can't order on line but they do mail-order.

**www.allaboutpartybags.co.uk**
Good: Great site easy to use, good selection.
Bad: home page could put you off.

**www.britishcandy.com**
Good: check out the jars section, you can buy old-fashioned sweets such as parma violets, sugar mice, space dust... great fun!
Bad: the home page is not very inviting, so please ignore that as the site is packed full of goodies.

**www.partydelights.co.uk**
Good: from piñatas to party bags and themed tableware for boys and girls. Deliver within 24 hours.
Bad: another dodgy home page... but the site is brilliant!

**www.partypieces.co.uk**
Good: this site thinks of everything to do with parties, very good price range and loads of fun ideas.
Bad: the design isn't great.

## Clothes

**www.showroom64.com**
Good: an incredible range of the most divine kids' clothes from babies to toddlers.
Bad: so much to choose from you could seriously damage your credit card.

### Fancy dress
**www.partydomain.co.uk**
Good: fantastic range of children's and toddlers' fancy dress outfits as well as personalised printed balloons.
Bad: garish design.

**www.bobandblossom.com**
Good: gorgeous site with fantastic gift ideas. Very easy to use.
Bad: nothing.

**www.mittyjames.com**
Good: the best towelling hooded tops online, very practical.
Bad: quite conservative.

**www.boden.co.uk**
Good: one of the best kids' sites; fantastic range for girls and boys.
Bad: your kids will look better than you do

**www.cookingapple.co.uk**
Good: old fashioned knitwear for children that is simply delicious.

Bad: more please. For baby clothes these are quite expensive...but they're handmade.

**www.tulipandnettle.co.uk**
Good: the most divine clothes on this site. The girls' range is to die for.
Bad: you need to order fast as they seem to run out of stock quite quickly.

**www.mynametags.com**
Good: Clever site where you can order your child's nametags. Very simple and easy to use.
Bad: the site is very basic.

## Education

**www.bbc.co.uk/schools**
Good: very informative site. This is for online learning and it is a fun way for kids to use the internet.
Bad: nothing, this entire site is fantastic.

## Home education

**www.heas.org.uk**
Good: this is a home education advisory service. You get sent a starter pack. This site is very helpful and simple to use.
Bad: annual subscription of £13.50.

## Primary schools

**www.ofsted.gov.uk**
Good: if you're looking for schools in your area just type in your postcode and the schools are listed. There is a registered list of childminders as well as all state and independent schools. A vital site.
Bad: not a particularly exciting site, but then again this is serious stuff!

## Interactive learning

**www.mousing.co.uk**
Good: simple interactive site that teaches your child to use a mouse.
Bad: so basic that there are only a few games.

**www.thebigbus.com**
Good: interactive learning site.
Bad: the site can be a bit temperamental.

## Web guides

**www.yahooligans.com**
Good: Amazing web guide for kids, safe and user friendly. There is so much to do and find on this site.
Bad: it could take over your kids' lives completely!

**www.all4kidsuk.com**
Good: amazing web directory with everything you need to find online. Very easy to use.
Bad: information overload.

**www.ajkids.com**
Good: play games and ask questions. A fantastic way for children to use the internet.
Bad: you won't be able to tear your kids away!

**www.gridclub.com**
Good: Amazing kids' site. Online learning and loads of fun.
Bad: the downside is you have to pay £29.99 to join!

**www.yucky.com**
Good: this may not be educational... but it's such a fun site for the yuckiest experiments! Fantastic on a rainy day.
Bad: be prepared for lots of mess!

## Storage

**www.gltc.co.uk**
Good: a brilliant site for storage and furniture. Check out the in-betweenee chair!
Bad: not the best design but we can live with that.

## Furniture

**www.thewhitecompany.com**
Good: dream-like furniture for kids and loads more.
Bad: you could get side tracked and end up shopping for yourself!

## Bedroom

**www.theholdingcompany.co.uk**
Good: fun cartoon storage boxes and different ideas.
Bad: not a huge amount of choice.

**www.letterbox.co.uk**
Good: loads of great storage ideas, including hanging pegs, drawers and much more.
Bad: busy home page that could put you off.

**www.dragonsofwaltonstreet.com**
Good: classic children's furniture. The painted monogrammed chair is a favourite.
Bad: you can't buy online, but they do mail-order via a catalogue

**www.monogrammedlinenshop.com**
good: beautiful traditional ideas, perfect for christening presents. Get a child's name mono-grammed on sheets, pillows or bathrobes.
Bad: not much, the site is very simple and not overwhelming.

## Gifts

**www.coolgiftsforkids.co.uk**
Good: such a sweet site for original gifts for all ages.
Bad: the site is a tad confusing to begin with, but once you get to grips with it it's fine.

**www.coxandcox.co.uk**
Good: go straight to the children's corner, there are the most heavenly ideas on this site.
Bad: not enough! We want more!

## Mother and baby

**www.mothercare.com**
Good: everything you need for you and your baby.
Bad: so much to choose from you could get lost.

**www.babycentre.co.uk**
Good: a site you can't live without if you are planning to get pregant or you are already pregnant. The most fantastic amount of information for all first-time mums.
Bad: nothing!

# entertainment

## Bookings

**www.ents24.com**
Good: amazing site for booking tickets online, loads of information. Totally safe.
Bad: they don't display all the gigs so you have to type in what you are looking for.

**www.ticketmaster.com**
Good: very efficient site, safe and reliable. You can buy pretty much any tickets here.
Bad: not the most exciting design.

**www.ticketweb.co.uk**
Good: the best site to buy tickets for gigs.
Bad: not much.

**www.easycinema.com**
Good: type in your postcode to find out which movies are playing in your area and book tickets. Very simple to use. You can also rent DVDs for £1.99! They post them to you and you post them back. So easy, it's untrue.
Bad: is that orange colour really necessary?

**www.cinemas-online.co.uk**
Good: listings of what's on at the movies in your area and you can book online. Easy to use.
Bad: not much. Really convenient.

**www.timeout.com**
Good: find out what's going in all the major cities.
Bad: a lot of information to surf through.

**www.aloud.com**
Good: brilliant online ticket service that's so easy to use. If you are travelling across the country to see a band, aloud.com have deals with loads of hotels (click 'sleeping' for a list).
Bad: too much choice.

**www.efestivals.co.uk**
Good: if you are a fan of festivals this is the perfect site for you. All the information possible on what's on. You can book online.
Bad: homepage is rather over-whelming.

**www.thisislondon.co.uk**
Good: all you'll ever need to know about the capital, where to go for good food, theatre, clubs, and bundles more. A fantastic site.
Bad: too much choice!

## Theatre

**www.theatrenet.com**
Good: everything to do with theatreland, really easy site to use with great links.
Bad: not much.

**www.officiallondontheatre.co.uk**
Good: in-depth write-ups on each play as well as info on how to get there. There is a great section for kids and where to take them.
Bad: the ads are slightly annoying.

## Days out

**www.chessington.com**
Good: fun day out at Chessington World of Adventures. Book your tickets online to save time. Loads of info about what you can do once you get there.
Bad: not much, it's good to plan ahead.

**www.londonpass.com**
Good: visit London Zoo and with this pass you get free entry to 50 other London attractions.
Bad: so much to see.

**www.woburnsafari.co.uk**
Good: this is an incredible day out. You can book tickets through the website and find out all you need to know before setting off.
Bad: not much. This is a very informative site.

**www.londoneye.com**
Good: book a trip to the London Eye and be blown away.
Bad: bit of a dull site.

**www.balloonflights.co.uk**
Good: go hot air ballooning in your area. Just click on the UK map and find out where the nearest trips are to you.
Bad: not the prettiest website.

**www.redletterdays.co.uk**
Good: brilliant site where you can get info about amazing days out. Definitely worth checking out.
Bad: you could become an adrenaline junkie.

**www.houseofmagic.co.uk**
Good: if you are looking for something different for a party, try the house of magic. Renowned magician Simon Drake will keep you spellbound.
Bad: the site looks quite dodgy.

**www.flights4all.com**
Good: amazing site for people who are potty about flying. Book a gliding lesson or learn how to fly a helicopter.
Bad: the homepage is so packed you may be put off.

**www.tribute-entertainment.co.uk**
Good: hilarious site with loads of lookalikes and tribute bands that you can hire for any event, such as weddings, birthdays, etc.
Bad: not much, pure entertainment.

**www.friendsinvited.com**
Good: fabulous service. Create your own party invitations. So much choice. very good prices.
Bad: not much.

**www.quintessentially.com**
Good: you need to be a member to use this exclusive service which brings you the best in arts, opera, music, travel and more.
Bad: so exclusive that you may not be accepted as a member.

## Art

**www.tate.org.uk**
Good: find out what's on at the Tate and you can book tickets online. Really great site with loads of information.
Bad: surprisingy, not the best designed site.

**www.artnet.com**
Good: for any art lover this is a fantastic site where you can find work by artists as well as art for sale.
Bad: you could get lost for hours on this site.

**www.whitecube.com**
Good: a site dedicated to art lovers. Check out what's on and view the artist's work online.
Bad: the site is well designed, but it doesn't always work properly.

**www.nationalgallery.org.uk**
Good: plan your visit through the site, which is really well thought out from maps of the floor plan to disability access. Everything you need to know is on here.
Bad: the site is a tad plain.

**www.royalacademy.org.uk**
Good: you can book tickets online and find out what exhibitions are on.
Bad: strangely modern site for such an old establishment.

**www.moma.org**
Good: great way to escape for a few hours and you don't have to go to New York! Brilliant site.
Bad: be prepared to surf for hours.

**www.louvre.fr**
Good: breathtaking art and culture on here, fabulous, informative and well thought-out site for art students and art lovers.
Bad: you need hours here.

## Restaurant guides

**www.zagat.com**
Good: arguably the best restaurant guide around. All major cities worldwide available.
Bad: the site is too high tech and complex. Keep it simple, we say!

**www.london-eating.co.uk**
Good: brilliant site. Just type in your postcode and the kind of food you are after and a list of places appears. Read the reviews section. Easy and simple to use.
Bad: not much, but it only finds London restaurants.

**www.theaa.co.uk**
Good: a wide choice of restaurants across the UK. Great layout.
Bad: you'll need a magnifying glass to see the restaurant link.

**www.routiers.co.uk**
Good: an eclectic choice of restaurants nationwide. A simple site that's easy to use.
Bad: you may pile on the pounds.

**www.toptable.co.uk**
Good: amazing site full of fab ideas for places to eat. You can also find out where to go in cities worldwide. The restaurant reviews are fun too.
Bad: site can be temperamental.

## TV and gossip

**www.abc.com**
Good: get a sneak preview of your favourite American TV shows and discover plots before anyone else.

Bad: spoilsports! We don't want to know the endings yet.

**www.bbc.co.uk/entertainment**
Good: loads of news, reviews on the world of entertainment and TV.
Bad: so much that you will get side tracked for hours!

**www.radiotimes.com**
Good: the godfather of TV guides, every channel imaginable is here.
Bad: you will become a tele-addict.

**www.onthebox.com**
Good: really cool site. Very simple with a clear view of what's on TV.
Bad: nothing.

**www.itv.com**
Good: check out all the news of your favourite shows. Loads of great stuff here.
Bad: not much, this is a fab site.

**www.channel4.com**
Good: all the news and gossip from your favourite shows. There is loads happening here, so get ready to get lost in cyber space.
Bad: highly addictive.

**www.thesmokinggun.com**
Good: gossip galore. Check out the mug-shot section! Great stories in the archive section too.
Bad: mainly geared to the US.

**www.hollywood.com**
Good: gossip central! Find out the ins and outs of tinsel town.
Bad: you'll get consumed by this site.

**www.eonline.com**
Good: all the movie and tinsel town gossip you could possibly need can be found right here. Plus what is happening on your favourite American TV shows.
Bad: not much, this is pure heaven.

# fashion

## Clothes

**www.topshop.co.uk**
Good: the Mecca! Fabulous site. So easy to shop and the returns policy is 30 days. The best bit on the site is topshop express: if you need something new for a party, place your order before 3 pm and it will be delivered to you that afternoon. Free delivery if you spend over £100.
Bad: highly addictive

**www.boden.co.uk**
Good: some of the best swimwear online. Very friendly site. Loads of choice.
Bad: some stock sells out fast so you have to wait to up to three weeks to receive your order. Plan ahead!

**www.my-wardrobe.com**
Good: new clothes site with fantastic labels. Clean and so user friendly. You'll love shopping here!
Bad: some sections are a little sparse.

**www.apc.fr**
Good: straight from Paris, APC has the most fab simple clothes, the site is very slick and easy to use, and they ship to the UK at a cost of 15 euros.
Bad: things tend to sell out fast. You need macromedia to play it.

**www.yoox.com**
Good: every label under the sun, this site is bursting with clothes.
Bad: very unclear…there is too much choice.

**www.net-a-porter.com**
Good: the mother of all fashion sites. The best collections online.
Bad: mainly for fashion victims with serious money to burn.

**www.frenchconnection.com**
Good: very high tech…check out the film. You can shop online too.
Bad: can be a bit full-on when you first enter it.

**www.laredoute.com**
Good: amazing online catalogue with thousands of items at really good prices, mainly French high-street labels. You need hours on this site!
Bad: too much choice.

**www.monsoon.co.uk**
Good: if you don't have a Monsoon in your area, this is the perfect way to shop.
Bad: the site is fairly basic.

**www.satineboutique.com**
Good: the fab LA shop that is online too. Although some labels are European they seem to have different collections out there. This site really has mouth-watering clothes. Fashionista's paradise!
Bad: shipping via Fedex will cost you $60.

**www.brownsfashion.com**
Good: this site may not be the prettiest of designs, but the brands they carry are fantastic, and ordering is simple and efficient.
Bad: most of the clothes are expensive.

**www.usastyle4u.com**
Good: great American buys that are finally available in the UK. The jeans are brilliant.
Bad: not much.

**www.toast.co.uk**
Good: truly gorgeous clothing online, and the site is so easy to use. Be aware that sizing can come up quite differently, but the exchange policy is very straightforward.

Bad: you could get seriously carried away.

**www.riverisland.com**
Good: very good layout, a slick site with lots of choice.
Bad: enormous amount of stuff to get through, you could spend a day here!

**www.whatsmineisyours.com**
Good: really clever site where you can sell or swap your clothes. Less daunting than eBay, but you have to pay a £5.00 joining fee.
Bad: when you first get on this site it can be really confusing. You need to read carefully how to buy and sell.

**www.notonthehighstreet.com**
Good: from clothes to pets and loads more. Really great stuff on this site.
Bad: products are expensive.

**www.moretvicar.com**
Good: brilliant T-shirts online. Great babygros too!
Bad: it'll take you hours to surf on here.

**www.selfridges.com**
Good: the graphics alone are fantastic, more of an informative site than any thing else.
Bad: you can't shop online or see any clothes here.

**www.cocoribbon.com**
Good: seriously yummy clothing! Very easy to use. Delivery the same day in London.
Bad: expensive, you could get seriously into debt.

**www.angeljackson.com**
Good: gorgeous accessories and handbags straight to your door! Oh, the joys of internet shopping!
Bad: some bits of the site don't work!

**www.brora.co.uk**
Good: delicious cashmere. Amazing site, and really easy to find your way around.
Bad: you could end up broke.

**www.ebay.co.uk**
Good: a revolutionary way to shop. Beyond highly addictive once you get into the swing of it.
Bad: be aware of fake items, not all ebayers are honest. You could end up filing for bankruptcy. Once you start you just can't stop!

**www.balenciaga.com**
Good: amazing photos of various collections and dream products.
Bad: information only, you can't buy online.

**www.dvflondon.com**
Good: buy a gorgeous Diane von Furstenberg dress on line. Great selection.
Bad: the pictures and quality of this site are not great.

**www.hoxtonboutique.co.uk**
Good: the ultimate cool site, amazing accessories and clothes from the cult shop.
Bad: you have to order over the phone.

**www.candccalifornia.com**
Good: the best T-shirts in the world. So many colours and styles! The choice is endless. Ships to the UK.
Bad: we know these are amazing, but they are over priced.

**www.marcjacobs.com**
Good: take a look at all the various collections online. You can't buy on here so you need to go to www.net-a-porter.com if you feel a burning desire to shop.
Bad: the site is too high tech and therefore a nightmare to use.

**www.chloe.com**
Good: the most gorgeous clothes ever! You can shop online – link straight to www.net-a-porter.com
Bad: not much.

**www.thecrossshop.com**
Good: the most gorgeous shop right at your fingertips. Check out the top ten items of the week.
Bad: highly addictive.

**www.dorothyperkins.co.uk**
Good: easy site to navigate, some real bargains. Check out the fashion advice for useful tips.
Bad: a bit on the bland side.

**www.johnsmedley.com**
Good: straightforward with no frills. Buy yummy sweaters online.
Bad: what a dreary site!

**www.littlewoods.com**
Good: brilliant. Everything from trainers to iPods. Terrific range of tops to suit every shape and a superb selection of lingerie, including our very own Trinny & Susannah Original Magic Knickers.
Bad: too much choice.

**www.odabash.com**
Good: sexy swimwear from Melissa Odabash. Check out the accessories too, the beach bags are brilliant.
Bad: not enough to choose from! The site could be a lot simpler.

**www.americanapparel.co.uk**
Good: the best T-shirts and cosy sweatshirts from this American label. Finally available in the UK. Hoorah!
Bad: so many colours, so many styles, it's easy to get confused.

**www.fashion.net**
Good: so chic, fantastic links to other sites.
Bad: quite pretentious.

## Lingerie

**www.sexypantiesandnaughtyknickers.com**
Good: (also known as 'spank') a divine collection of gorgeous underwear. You can order online and they have large sizes.
Bad: the bra range is not for the big boobed.

**www.figleaves.com**
Good: the best online lingerie ever! There is so much choice and you can shop by your size. They go up to large bra sizes and you can buy maternity bras too. Delivery is quick.
Bad: a little overwhelming as there is so much to choose from.

**www.agentprovocateur.com**
Good: the sexiest underwear you can buy. They have a fab new maternity collection. Very saucy site!
Bad: expensive.

**www.rigbyandpeller.com**
Good: fantastic selection of underwear, they are renowned for their bras.
Bad: the site is a little confusing. Expensive.

**www.marksandspencer.com**
Good: M&S never lets you down! There is a clever chart on how to measure your breast size at home! Considering that 85% of women do not wear their correct bra size, this is brilliant! Especially if you are a too self-conscious to go and have your measurements taken by a stranger.
Bad: nothing – it's M&S.

**www.bodas.co.uk**
Good: gorgeous range of everyday underwear. Very affordable as well.
Bad: not enough of a selection.

**www.mytights.com**
Good: tights heaven, basically an online tights supermarket.
Bad: you'll get absorbed in tights world.

**www.wolfordboutiquelondon.com**
Good: arguably the best tights available. Great site with loads of choice and the best colours.
Bad: at times it doesn't work properly.

## Shoes

**www.georginagoodman.com**
Good: beautiful site for beautiful shoes! These are truly bespoke shoes, indulge yourself and buy them online!
Bad: too much choice – you will want them all.

**www.gina.com**
Good: gorgeous site, the shoes look fabulous on here! Perfect for all shoe addicts. They deliver worldwide.
Bad: expensive habit to develop.

**www.jimmychoo.com**
Good: beautiful site, the photos alone will inspire you to buy a pair of shoes! You can email your order and they send the shoes out to you via the nearest shop.
Bad: you may need to re-mortgage.

**www.kurtgeiger.com**
Good: great selection of shoes from highs to flats, something for everybody.
Bad: you could damage your credit card.

**www.schuhstore.co.uk**
Good: online 'supermarket' for shoes and trainers. Delivery is fast and efficient.
Bad: you could end up buying something just for the sake of it.

**www.vivaladiva.com**
Good: lots of different brands to choose from.
Bad: rather confusing site.

**www.birkenstock.co.uk**
Good: pure sandal heaven.
Bad: the design isn't great.

**www.havaianasdirect.co.uk**
Good: the best flip-flops in the world. So comfy you'll want them in every colour. Delivers anywhere in the UK.
Bad: appalling design.

## Accessories

**www.sunglassesuk.com**
Good: huge choice of designer sunglasses at great prices, check out their celeb finder.
Bad: some glasses don't have large images so it's hard to know what you're buying.

**www.inedite.net**
Good: fab items from Brazil and Mexico. Really refreshing to find things that are different!
Bad: not the best looking site, but who cares.

**www.kabiri.co.uk**
Good: some truly amazing jewellery from up-and-coming designers.

Bad: not enough selection, we want more.

**www.mikeyjewellery.co.uk**
Good: cheap and cheerful jewellery, loads of great pieces, brilliant for gifts.
Bad: not much.

**www.accessorize.co.uk**
Good: accessories galore! Everything you need to jazz up an outfit. Really great prices. The iPod cases are fabulous.
Bad: so much choice you may end up spending more than you bargained for.

**www.luluguinness.com**
Good: fab design, great bags and accessories. So much choice you will definitely find what you are looking for.
Bad: quite expensive.

**www.bottegaveneta.com**
Good: mouthwateringly beautiful site, the images are fantastic.
Bad: you can only buy online if you live in the US...boo, hoo!

**www.anyahindmarch.com**
Good: order your own personal photo bag online.
Bad: not enough choice.

**www.tattydevine.com**
Good: fabulous accessories that have a tongue-in-cheek

approach to fashion.
Bad: you have to email your order through which can be a bit confusing.

**www.butlerandwilson.co.uk**
Good: the most gorgeous jewellery – you will be spoilt for choice. It's a clever site too as it shows you the last items you have viewed.
Bad: the home page looks a bit iffy, but ignore that and surf away.

## Magazines

**www.trinnyandsusannah.com**
Good: get loads of top Trinny and Susannah tips on how to dress for your body shape, what colours to wear and everything that's happening in our world. We promise we won't come round to your house and grab your boobs.
Bad: it's like having US sitting in your living room – scary.

**www.dailycandy.com**
Good: online magazine with fab articles on what's hot and happening in various cities around the world. The graphics are to die for.
Bad: you will get hooked and need a daily dose.

**www.vogue.co.uk**
Good: dedicated to every fashionista out there. So full of goodies you will spend hours here!
Bad: not much.

**www.graziamagazine.co.uk**
Good: the best gossip and fashion rolled into one, with amazing goodie bags to be won.
Bad: not much!

**www.harpersandqueen.co.uk**
Good: tons of fabulous fashion

and articles. Also great sections on restaurants and travel.
Bad: not the best design which is surprising considering this is such a fab mag.

**www.condenast.co.uk**
Good: check out all the magazines you love from Condé Nast.
Bad: sometimes the site doesn't work properly.

**www.popbitch.com**
Good: more gossip than fashion, but somehow these two go hand in hand. Brilliant stories and loads more.
Bad: beyond addictive!

**www.hintmag.com**
Good: the best online fashion magazine. If you are a dedicated fashion lover then you will not be able to survive without hint mag.
Bad: not much.

**We also thank the following labels which appear in this book**

All Saints:
**www.allsaints.co.uk**
Aquascutum:
**www.aquascutum.co.uk**
Ben de Lisi:
**www.bendelisi.com**
Coast:
**www.coast-stores.co.uk**
Collette Dinnigan:
**www.collettedinnigan.com.au**
Damaris:
**www.damaris-london.com**
Dolce & Gabbana:
**www.dolcegabbana.it**
Fenn Wright Manson:
**www.fennwrightmanson.com**
George at Asda:
**www.george.com**
Gharani Strok:
**www.gharanistrok.co.uk**
Hilfiger:
**www.tommy.com**
Issa, available at Browns:

**www.brownsfashion.com**
Jenny Dyer:
**jennydyerlondon.com**
Joseph:
**www.joseph.co.uk**
Karen Millen:
**www.karenmillen.com**
Luisa Beccaria:
**www.luisabeccaria.it**
Liz Claibone:
**www.lizclaiborne.com**
Marni:
**www.marni.com**
Matthew Williamson:
**www.matthewwilliamson.com**
Missoni:
**www.missoni.com**
Mk One:
**www.mkone.co.uk**
New Look:
**www.newlook.co.uk**
Peacocks:
**www.peacocks.co.uk**
Prada:
**www.prada.com**
Principles:
**www.principles.co.uk**
Roland Mouret:
**www.rolandmouretshowroom.co.uk**
7 for all mankind:
**www.7forallmankind.com**
Speedo:
**www.speedo.com**
Sticky Fingers:
**www.sticky-fingers.co.uk**
Sweaty Betty:
**www.sweatybetty.com**
Temperley:
**www.temperleylondon.com**
Tk Maxx:
**www.tkmaxx.com**
Wallis:
**www.wallis-fashion.com**
Zara:
**www.zara.com**

# food

## Online food stores

**www.ocado.com**
Good: the best online food delivery service. This site will literally transform your life. Perfect for stay-at-home mums. Very easy to use. Free delivery if you spend over £75.00.
Bad: can't book a delivery slot more than a month in advance

**www.sainsburys.co.uk**
Good: excellent site. When you click on a product it gives all the information about the product, its contents and how to prepare it – vital for allergy sufferers.
Bad: there is a £5.00 delivery charge.

**www.tesco.com**
Good: user friendly. For the express shopper service, simply type out your list and let them run around the aisles for you!
Bad: not much.

**www.goodnessdirect.co.uk**
Good: amazing health super-market with macrobiotic and gluten free food and organic produce. This is truly a fab site.
Bad: almost too healthy!

**www.formanandfield.com**
Good: about the best smoked salmon in the world. This is a seriously luxurious site.
Bad: some of the products are quite expensive, but if you're going to buy caviar what do you expect?

**www.fortnumandmason.com**
Good: the products alone will make you drool. Very easy site to get around. Deliciousness at your fingertips.
Bad: you could end up spending a small fortune!

**www.cybercandy.co.uk**
Good: order all your favourite candy, from everywhere from the States to Japan and tons more.
Bad: not for health freaks

**www.thorntons.co.uk**
Good: great site with loads of brilliant ideas such as chocolate hampers – what a great thing to send someone! There are even diabetic products available.
Bad: looks a bit old fashioned.

**www.farmersmarkets.net**
Good: find out where your local farmers' market is.
Bad: not much else on this site. It's info only.

**www.first4fruit.com**
Good: a genius idea – send a hamper of fresh fruit as a gift, there's lots to choose from.
Bad: there isn't anything.

**www.homegrowndirect.com**
Good: fresh fruit and veg delivery service. Nothing is more than 48 hours old on this site.
Bad: not much.

**www.thefishsociety.co.uk**
Good: get fish delivered to your door. Check out the sushi section, it's simply delicious.
Bad: free delivery only if you spend over £100!!!

**www.fromages.com**
Good: French cheese delivered within 24hours. The ultimate site for cheese lovers.
Bad: most prices are in Euros.

**www.lamaisonduchocolat.com**
Good: the most divine chocolate! Very slick site, the pictures are so clear you can almost taste it.
Bad: not much, a truly fab site.

## Specialist diets

Coeliac products
**www.crayves.co.uk**
Good: yummy gluten-free products.
Bad: the downside is that you can't order online.

Wheat and dairy free
**www.wheatanddairlyfree.com**
Good: brilliant online shop for those intolerant to wheat and dairy. Varied range of products.
Bad: not much.

Organics
**www.organicfood.co.uk**
Good: great directory with all the information and links to the best organic sites around.
Bad: nothing.

## Cooking

**www.deliaonline.com**
Good: great website with very useful tips – she even teaches you how to boil an egg. There are also great recipes for people who are allergic to nuts, gluten, etc.
Bad: not much.

**www.ichef.com**
Good: hundreds of delicious recipes at the click of your mouse.
Bad: the advert banners will drive you insane.

**www.jamieoliver.com**
Good: such a great site and the recipes are very easy to follow.
Bad: not enough choice though.

**www.bbc.co.uk/food**
Good: brilliantly informative site with a lot of choice and interesting recipes with exact cooking and preparation times which is very useful. It's healthy too.
Bad: nothing.

**www.agalinks.co.uk**
Good: brilliant online recipes that take you through the whole process step by step.
Bad: you may pile on the pounds.

**www.bestbritishfood.co.uk**
Good: loads of recipes for your favourite British food. You can email your own recipes to them and they put them online for others to share. Not all 'cheffy' and professional.
Bad: site design is pretty basic.

## Nutritionist

**www.thefooddoctor.com**
Good: lots of information! You can buy the yummy seed mix pots online...great snacks.
Bad: you could end up spending a fortune!

## Healthy eating

**www.eattheseasons.co.uk**
Good: fantastic site that tells you which foods are in season and why you should eat them.
Bad: could take the fun out of food.

## Wine

**www.surf4wine.co.uk**
Good: check out the wine matcher – this will tell you which wine to drink with which food.
Bad: information overload.

**www.winecellar.co.uk**
Good: great site for wine lovers – you can buy your wine by the grape variety. The site is very easy to use. If you are not a wine connoisseur don't panic, there is plenty of information and help.
Bad: not much.

## Tips and hygiene

**www.foodlink.org.uk**
Good: educational site with inter-active games and tips. Very easy to use and informative. Complete guide to food safety.
Bad: not much.

**www.foodfriend.co.uk**
Good: simply type in your email address and the food friend will email or text you three clever tips a week. For example, if you're stressed then eat an avocado. Very useful tips.
Bad: after a while the texts might drive you mad.

## Online movie

**www.storewars.org**
Good: amazing online movie about organic products made like Star Wars. You have to watch this!
Bad: can't think of anything.

# health

## Advice/Care

**www.embarrassingproblems.co.uk**
Good: fantastic advice and information as well as links to specific sites about particular problems. You never need feel embarrassed again!
Bad: not much.

**www.allcures.com**
Good: online doctors, pharmacy, beauty. You can register and get online advice and shop online.
Bad: almost too much information…but is that a bad thing?

**www.patient.co.uk**
Good: very informative site to do with healthcare, great tips and site links.
Bad: so much information that you can get lost and wander off into total hypochondria.

**www.pms.org.uk**
Good: loads of invaluable info regarding PMS, tips to help you each month as well as a whole range of alternative treatments.
Bad: there is an awful lot to get through!

**www.caloriecounter.co.uk**
Good: calculate your food intake – a fab list adds up how much you should eat in a day. You won't go hungry. They do not encourage crash diets.
Bad: could make you obsessive.

**www.menopausematters.co.uk**
Good: an amazing site for such a personal issue. You can find out all you need to know in the privacy of your own home. There is a forum where you can chat to other women too.
Bad: not a lot, this site works very well.

**www.cancerresearchuk.org**
Good: a truly fantastic site, there is so much information and help available here.
Bad: nothing.

**www.womens-health.co.uk**
Good: purely dedicated to women's health issues, highly informative and really useful. There are also some very good links to other related sites.
Bad: quite a depressing design.

**www.bbc.co.uk/health/womens_health**
Good: yet another fabulous site from the BBC, this really is a true joy to surf around. There's lots of important and spot-on info about women's health.
Bad: not much.

**www.health-fitness-tips.com**
Good: simple, straightforward and helpful tips. There isn't too much information being slung at you, which is actually rather refreshing.
Bad: the design is so boring that you may fall asleep.

**www.quackwatch.com**
Good: loads of insight into fake vitamin pushers and bogus facts.
Bad: sadly the layout of this site is super confusing so you really need to persist with it.

**www.streetdrugs.org**
Good: a really well presented site that helps parents to become aware if their kids are on drugs. It lists the behaviours to look out for.
Bad: nothing, this is a really important site.

**www.postoptics.co.uk**
Good: have your lenses delivered to your door, so much cheaper than most opticians.
Bad: too much faffing about when it comes to the checkout.

## Doctors

**www.surgerydoor.co.uk**
Good: great section on emergencies and what to do, loads of info on medical conditions and fantastic advice for parents who think their children may be on drugs. A vital site.
Bad: nothing apparent.

**www.netdoctor.co.uk**
Good: ask a doctor anything online: the layout is so simple that it's a joy to use!
Bad: you could become an obsessive doctor stalker.

**www.24dr.com**
Good: brilliant service – you can chat to a doctor from your computer!
Bad: you have to pay for an online consultation.

**www.nhsdirect.nhs.uk**
Good: vital site, very easy to use, lots of advice, and you can find out where your nearest NHS surgery is.
Bad: a lot of surgeries are full.

**www.samedaydoctor.co.uk**
Good: you can book an appointment for the same day.
Bad: it is expensive.

**www.dr.lockie.com**
Good: everything you need to know about homeopathy, very easy to use.
Bad: not much.

## Dentists

**www.dentalwisdom.com**
Good: all you need to know about teeth.
Bad: doesn't mean you can avoid going to the dentist!

**www.thedentalclinic.com**
Good: you can find a dentist in your area and book an appointment.
Bad: not much.

**www.londonsmiling.com**
Good: a routine examination is £25.00. Dentists are expensive, but this seems very reasonable.
Bad: only available in London.

**www.thesmileplace.co.uk**
Good: fantastic site. If you are conscious of the colour of your teeth when you smile this is the site for you! First you receive a kit to make the impressions of your teeth, you send it back (freepost) and then you receive your teeth whitening kit. All this for £99.00!
Bad: nothing!

## Yoga/Fitness

**www.agoy.com**

Good: you can buy yoga mats and DVDs online.
Bad: lacks information, would be great if you could learn a few yoga movements from the site but you can't. Products are rather expensive.

**www.thefitmap.com**
Good: amazing amount of info on health and exercise, great links to

other health sites. This is a portal.
Bad: there is so much to choose from that it is quite overwhelming.

**www.yogauk.com**
Good: brilliant site. There is a list of yoga teachers throughout the UK and there are fantastic links to other yoga-related sites.
Bad: the design of the site may put you off, but persevere – it's well worth it.

**www.thebodydoctor.com**
Good: if you are willing to get into shape this is an amazing way to do it. You can order the book and DVD and work out from home.
Bad: tough to maintain the programme on one's own.

**www.netfit.co.uk**
Good: finally a great site that shows you which exercises you can do. You can choose which part of your body you'd like to work on. Check out the 99 health tips.
Bad: not much.

## Massage/Pampering

**www.perfectlyathome.com**
Good: the height of luxury. Pamper yourself at home and book a massage.
Bad: quite expensive and only available in London.

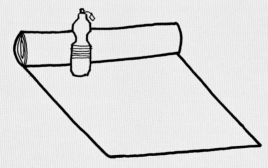

**www.unlistedlondon.com**
Good: bespoke service for at-home pampering.
Bad: so exclusive that the prices are high.

**www.thepamperparty.co.uk**
Good: great for hen or girly nights, from pedicures to massages. The prices are so reasonable. Available nationwide.
Bad: not much.

## Vitamins and Health Supplements

**www.healthspan.co.uk**
Good: order your vitamins online. Great site to use, very easy to order. Free postage and packaging.
Bad: not much.

**www.thinknatural.com**
Good: natural health at your fingertips, you can click on conditions and find a natural remedy for your ailment.
Bad: nothing at all.

**www.boots.com**
Good: the ever-reliable Boots direct to your door, loads of choice.
Bad: homepage is a bit messy and confusing.

**www.greensfoods.co.uk**
Good: vitamins galore! Such a great range of natural remedies.
Bad: you could end up spending a fortune.

**www.pharmacy2u.co.uk**
Good: how great to be able to buy your products online. Really fantastic site with an amazing range of products for everything imaginable.
Bad: nothing... this is a revolutionary site.

# home & recycling

## Utilities

**www.uswitch.com**
Good: find out if you are paying too much on your utility bills and save money! You can switch online, it's easy and a real eye opener.
Bad: nothing about saving money is a bad thing.

**www.energylinx.co.uk**
Good: compare your bills with other companies and see if you are being over charged. Very simple site.
Bad: you can't change suppliers on this site.

**www.good-energy.co.uk**
Good: switch to a supplier who supplies electricity only from 100% renewable sources.
Bad: saving the planet can only be good!

**www.corgi-gas-safety.com**
Good: find a gas installer near you. Important information on safety and general gas use.
Bad: nothing.

## Household

**www.hints-n-tips.com**
Good: terrific site that is full of amazing tips from people around the world who just email their hints and tips. Really useful and fun!
Bad: pretty basic design.

**www.sparekeys.com**
Good: brilliant site. You give sparekeys your details and they hold on to a set of your keys, so if you are locked out you can call them 24/7 and they will sort you out! A yearly membership fee is only £29.00. Much cheaper than calling out a locksmith.

Bad: not much, the site is simple to use.

**www.locksmiths.co.uk**
Good: find a locksmith nation-wide.
Bad: you are unlikely to have convenient internet access when you're locked out of your house.

**www.matren.co.uk/electricians**
Good: UK wide directory of electricians in your area.
Bad: boring site, but vital!

**www.safe-and-secure.uk.com**
Good: got an emergency? When you need a plumber, glazier, electrician or locksmith, type in your phone number and they get straight back to you.
Bad: very basic site. No price quotes online – you have to wait for them to call you.

**www.imperialplumbing.co.uk**
Good: 24-hour call out and there is a section on emergencies which gives you step-by-step instructions on how to turn off the water supply in case of a burst pipe.
Bad: not much.

## Recycling and green stuff

**www.recycleforlondon.com**
Good: if we all recycled what a difference we would make to our precious planet. This site offers loads of help on how to recycle. When you read the figures on how much waste London alone produces a year it's alarming.
Bad: nothing at all.

**www.freecycle.org**
Good: find your local group to give away or exchange things you don't want – and get stuff free!

Bad: it's quite tedious going through all the lists to find your local freecycle site.

**www.recyclenow.com**
Good: loads of tips on how to start recycling. Enter your post-code and find out how recycling works in your area and whether the council collects your recycled rubbish.
Bad: not much, the site is easy to use.

**www.anyjunk.co.uk**
Good: great service for house clearances, garden waste or any junk you want to get rid of.
Bad: only available in certain parts of London.

**www.ecojunk.com**
Good: great idea – they collect your junk and recycle a large percentage of it. The rest goes to charity.
Bad: only available in certain parts of London.

**www.lowimpact.org**
Good: you have heard about solar energy and biodiesel, but how do you get hold of them? The Low Impact Living Initiative has fact-sheets to help.
Bad: website is very worthy and boring.

**www.cat.org.uk**
Good: learn to build your own eco-house at the Centre for Alternative Technology or just shop online in the green shop.
Bad: design is uninspiring. You could fall asleep in the green shop.

**www.fishonline.org**
Good: find out if the fish you're buying is sustainably caught.
Bad: depressing number of species on the 'fish to avoid' list.

# DIY

## www.diy.com
Good: B&Q online, great ideas at reasonable prices, and you can shop online.
Bad: possibly too much choice.

## www.hometips.com
Good: entirely dedicated to DIY and home improvement, there are fantastic tips and advice as well as links to other sites.
Bad: you could get lost with the amount of information.

## www.diytools.com
Good: DIY heaven! Loads of tools for sale, lots of discounts, well worth looking at.
Bad: not the prettiest site, but that's not really the point. It's all about the tools.

## www.screwfixdirect.com
Good: tools at trade prices, join their chat rooms to discuss power tools and builder stuff!
Bad: nothing, if DIY is your thing, then this could be your idea of paradise.

## www.diyfixit.co.uk
Good: very easy to use, this site explains how to do DIY in such a simple way that you will be able to take on most tasks. The graphics are fun too. Great tips.
Bad: some pages seem to be unavailable.

## www.hss.co.uk
Good: to hire tools, just enter your postcode to find the nearest store to you. You can also open an account on line. They will deliver your hire equipment or you can pick it up.
Bad: they charge postage.

## www.homebase.co.uk
Good: all the varied DIY and household stuff you'd expect.
Bad: looking at the website is almost as exhausting as going to Homebase.

## www.homedoctor.net
Good: lots of basic DIY info.
Bad: much of the information is very basic indeed.

## www.dulux.co.uk
Good: you can order colour swatches and calculate how much paint you will need to cover the area you are painting. Make up your own scrapbook with all the colours you want.
Bad: sadly, you can't order the paint online.

## www.farrow-ball.co.uk
Good: wonderful paints and wallpaper, and you can order samples. The site is easy to use and has a fantastic range.
Bad: when ordering wallpaper, make sure you are 100% certain of what you are buying, as it is non-returnable.

## www.firedearth.co.uk
Good: mouthwatering products, from paint to furniture.
Bad: expensive.

## www.grahamandgreen.co.uk
Good: brilliant site with many fab ideas for the home as well as presents. A real treasure trove.
Bad: the site is a wee bit messy.

## www.salvo.co.uk
Good: excellent portal to many UK architectural salvage businesses and info on fairs, plus details of forthcoming demolitions.
Bad: it takes a long time to visit all the different websites.

## www.handlesdirect.co.uk
Good: handles galore.
Bad: disorganised website. You have to look in several different places so it's difficult to see choices of handles side-by-side.

# Home wares

## www.thewhitecompany.com
Good: superb bed linens and towels delivered to your door.
Bad: nothing.

## www.johnlewis.com
Good: lots of super-useful John Lewis wares to buy online.
Bad: unlike Ocado, you can't choose a 2-hour delivery slot, but are expected to hang around all day.

## www.cphart.co.uk
Good: cutting-edge designer bathrooms.
Bad: you can't find out the price of anything.

## www.lauraashley.com
Good: some truly gorgeous items to be found here! Easy site to use.
Bad: presentation is a bit twee.

## www.ikea.com
Good: find out if the things you want are actually in stock at your local branch.
Bad: no buying online – you still have to go to Ikea.

## www.argos.co.uk
Good: shop and pay online and pick it up from your nearest store.
Bad: confusing site

## www.pussyhomeboutique.co.uk
Good: funky house style items from sofas to cocktail sticks.
Bad: your home could end up looking like a fashion student's gaff.

**www.cathkidston.co.uk**
Good: gorgeous and quirky items for every room in the house in signature Cath Kidston pastel and floral prints.
Bad: your house might get so full of floral print knick-knacks that you have to move out and live in the Cath Kidston floral-print tent!

**www.europebynet.com**
Good: buy contemporary designer furniture at discount prices.
Bad: site could look more stylish.

**www.cologneandcotton.net**
Good: beautiful linens and the most divine selection of room fragrances and scented candles.
Bad: pricey.

**www.scp.co.uk**
Good: stunning contemporary furniture.
Bad: can't buy online and many prices are not listed.

**www.heals.co.uk**
Good: excellent range of modern furniture and useful home wares.
Bad: delivery times seem a bit vague.

**www.habitat.net**
Good: see all the latest funky Habitat stuff from home.
Bad: can't buy online. Too many confusing menus.

**www.mujionline.co.uk**
Good: organise your life! Buy all the fabulous Muji boxes and drawers online.
Bad: items are all over the place and difficult to find.

**www.therugcompany.co.uk**
Good: see lots of lovely rugs at home and imagine how they would look in your room.
Bad: colour reproduction is not great.

**www.retailjunky.com**
Good: loads of mad gadgets and gifts.
Bad: do you really need a smoking donkey or a Jesus action figure?

**www.conranshop.co.uk**
Good: everything you need for chic urban living.
Bad: deep pockets required.

**www.wallacesacks.com**
Good: Lovely cushions, vases and bits and bobs to jazz up your home.
Bad: website design is quite bland.

## Garden

**www.gardenseeker.com**
Good: nifty site with a great guide to pruning shrubs, and lists of garden centres and services nationwide.
Bad: nothing, this is the work of a committed enthusiast.

**www.english-nature.org.uk**
Good: gives guidance and fact-sheets on creating a nature garden.
Bad: great info but boring site. Needs more photos of plants and flowers.

**www.gardenzone.info**
Good: a simple site with straight-forward advice about growing organic herbs and vegetables.
Bad: long list of a menu makes it tedious to find the page you want.

**www.readersheds.co.uk**
Good: you've heard of Readers' Wives...see photos of other people's garden sheds.
Bad: everyone thinks their own shed is the sexiest.

**www.theurbangarden.co.uk**
Good: well-designed, interesting selection of garden accessories.
Bad: website has too many headings.

## Home organisers

**www.clutterclinic.co.uk**
Good: amazing service that comes and de-clutters your home. Available in London, the Southeast and Northern Ireland. The site is very well designed.
Bad: not much.

**www.unflatpack.co.uk**
Good: they will go to Ikea for you, bring you your order and even put it all together – for a fee.
Bad: if you order the Ikea meat-balls or hotdogs they'll probably be cold by the time they get to you.

**www.buy-time.co.uk**
Good: cash rich but time poor? Buy Time provides helpers to do your shopping and organise your life.
Bad: mostly in London.

## Buying a house

**www.primelocation.com**
Good: search and compare many properties in your area, see photos and floorplans without wasting time traipsing out to properties that don't meet your needs.
Bad: just like a real estate agent, this website will show you places you didn't ask to see.

**www.upmystreet.com**
Good: get your neighbourhood profile. Find out crime rates and how many of your neighbours have satellite TV – fascinating.
Bad: even more detail would be great.

# pets

## Pet insurance

**www.sainsburysbankpet.co.uk**
Good: straightforward site to get pet health care insurance. One of the cheapest insurers on the market.
Bad: price rockets if your pet is over eight years old.

**www.petprotect.co.uk**
Good: really good pet health care insurers. Easy to use – type in your details and they give you a quote.
Bad: rates soar if your pet is over eight years old.

**www.pethealthcare.com**
Good: all about pet health care and you can get insurance here as well. Very informative site with good links. The breed section is fantastic and tells you everything from the breeder's details to which food your pet should eat.
Bad: the Ask the Expert section never seems able to answer your questions!

## Quarantine laws

**www.defra.gov.uk/animalh/quarantine**
Good: everything you need to know about the pet travel scheme and the quarantine laws that apply to the UK.
Bad: not the best design, but that's not really the point!

## Breeders/TrainersVets

**www.myidealpuppy.com**
Good: new site dedicated to training your puppy. They also have a housesitting service, dog walkers and organic homemade treats. You can sign up for puppy-training classes. A really great service
Bad: only available in certain parts of London.

**www.trainyourpuppy.co.uk**
Good: the perfect site for those of you who don't want to have to go to training class. All the info you need is on this site, from toilet training to socialisation. Links available for puppy classes.
Bad: not much.

**www.the-kennel-club.org.uk**
Good: packed full of information on breeds, training and more.
Bad: some links seem a tad irrelevant. Not the most user-friendly site.

**www.dogs.co.uk**
Good: everything you need to know about dogs from breeders to trainers.
Bad: information overload.

**www.moggies.co.uk**
Good: to all you cat lovers out there – this site was made for you. There is a page dedicated to kittens and how to raise them. Well worth looking at.
Bad: quite a basic design.

**www.vetlist.co.uk**
Good: helps you find a vet in your area. Just type in your post code and you will find your nearest vet. Nationwide.
Bad: nothing, this is a simple site with no gimmicks.

## Animal rescue centres

**www.batterseadogshome.org.uk**
Good: lovely site, great design and very easy to use.
Bad: you will want to rescue every single animal on here.

**www.dogstrust.org.uk**
Good: if you are looking to rescue a dog, here is the site for you. You can also sponsor a dog. The site is easy to use and you can find a re-homing centre in your area.
Bad: heart wrenching!

**www.rspca.org**
Good: fab site for animal lovers. There is loads of information on how to help and protect animals from cruelty and a section on how to become a volunteer.
Bad: nothing at all.

## Beds/Accessories

**www.petplanet.co.uk**
Good: everything you need for your pets can be found on here! You can even chat to a vet online through the member's area.
Bad: you could get obsessed!

**www.lovemydog.biz**
Good: the best dog products ever! It's really hard to find good dog beds and collars. Look no further – this site rocks!
Bad: quite expensive but worth it.

**www.thedogboutique.co.uk**
Good: amazing site dedicated to your beloved pooch, really nice products too. The prices start from £3.00 up to £600.
Bad: nothing, this site is fabulous.

**www.llbean.com**
Good: this American site has fab pet beds. Type pets into the search engine and choose a bed, you can get your dog's name monogrammed on the cover. Shipping costs £11.00. Worth it.
Bad: delivery is up to three weeks.

**www.patchandscott.com**
Good: the chicest dog site around: the collars are mouthwateringly beautiful, and the leather beds are gorgeous!
Bad: very expensive.

# news, weather & finance

## News

**www.newsnow.co.uk**
Good: fantastic up-to-date news and current affairs. This site is constantly being updated with the latest news. Very easy to navigate.
Bad: you could literally spend hours and hours on this!

**www.sky.com**
Good: perfect site for you to be in the know about all the day's news.
Bad: not much.

**www.ananova.co.uk**
Good: a parent company of Orange, this site is great. The design is simple, there are no banners all over the place, and it's so clean and to the point. Catch up with all the day's news.
Bad: nothing springs to mind.

**www.thepaperboy.com**
Good: read through the papers worldwide. Just click on the paper you want to read and you go straight to their site.
Bad: can be confusing at first.

**www.anorak.co.uk**
Good: if you love the tabloids, this site is for you. All the best bits are here. You can even search their archives and find old stories. Great site!
Bad: not very high brow!

**www.bbc.co.uk**
Good: one of the best online news sites. So much information, full weather section and loads more.
Bad: you could get lost in surfing land.

**www.reuters.co.uk**
Good: straightforward, no-nonsense breaking news site!
Bad: nothing.

**www.davesdaily.com**
Good: hilarious site with some of the weirdest news stories around.
Bad: mainly American stories, but well worth looking at.

**www.thesun.co.uk**
Good: great site with all the news and gossip you could ever need.
Bad: nothing – this is highly addictive reading!

## Weather

**www.met-office.gov.uk**
Good: very thorough site dedicated to the weather.
Bad: you may become obsessed with the weather!

**www.climateark.org**
Good: all about climate change and global warming… scary but very informative.
Bad: quite confusing at first.

**www.bbc.co.uk/weather**
Good: fantastic site, very simple and easy to use with up-to-date information on the weather.
Bad: nothing!

**www.spaceweather.com**
Good: amazing site that tells you what's up weather-wise in space. OK, it may not be vital, but it's really fascinating!
Bad: no earth forecasts.

**www.stormstock.com**
Good: some incredible pictures taken of major storms, well worth checking out.
Bad: not much.

## Finance

**www.moneyfacts.co.uk**
Good: all you need to know about finances, clear advice on mortgages, loans and credit cards.
Bad: you could be tempted to get more cards than you need!

**www.moneysavingexpert.com**
Good: genius site with so many tips on how to save and get the best value for your money. A real beginner's guide to financial manageability.
Bad: so much information to get through!

**www.xe.com**
Good: currency converter. So easy to use, you'll get hooked!
Bad: not much.

**www.onlinefx.com**
Good: order your travel money online. Currency conversion as well as international money transfers.
Bad: not the most thrilling site but very useful.

**www.caxtonfx.com**
Good: great site that deals in personal or business finance matters such as trusts, emigration, tax issues and investments. Very easy to use.
Bad: not much

## Online banking

### www.firstdirect.com
Good: welcome to online banking at its best, easy to use and so practical you need never go and queue in a bank again. Revolutionary!
Bad: impersonal, but how great to be in control of your finances from home.

### www.smile.co.uk
Good: here you have the freedom to check out the state of your current account 24 hours a day seven days a week! Fantastic rates, well worth a visit.
Bad: not much.

### www.banksafeonline.org.uk
Good: brilliant site to help you stay safe online. Loads of tips about online banking and scams – pretty vital in this day and age. Helpful links to other safe sites.
Bad: not much, as you can never be too careful.

### www.paypal.com
Good: the secure online payment service for Internet shopping. Very simple to use, most ebay users only accept paypal.
Bad: you could end up spending loads of money on the net as it's so easy to use!

### www.fool.co.uk
Good: loads of tips and help with financial decisions. Choose a mortgage or credit card, compare rates. Really good site.
Bad: quite confusing at first, you don't really know what's going on until you start searching.

## Debt

### www.debtorsanonymous.org.uk
Good: based on the twelve-step recovery program this is a fantastic way to help sort out your debt problems. There is a list of meetings nationwide.
Bad: nothing, this can only work to your advantage.

### www.thedebtpeople.co.uk
Good: very comprehensive site for people to clear their debts, just pop in your details and they will get back to you.
Bad: you can't get answers online. Like most debt repayments schemes it takes 60 months for your debt to clear... you do the maths!

# teenagers

## Safety first

Please be careful while using chat rooms: never ever give out your real name, address or phone number. Do not agree to meet up with someone you have met over the internet. Be aware that some people may not be who they say they are.

## Fashion

**www.fredflare.com**
Good: fabulous site from the US. Check out the music boom box and play tunes while you surf around. They do ship to the UK. Great fashion too.
Bad: you will become totally hooked!

**www.oki-ni.com**
Good: slick, cutting edge and underground, this is for the serious fashionista. Most products are unique to oki-ni.
Bad: expensive.

**www.topshop.com**
Good: the best site on the planet for shopping, essential for all you cool cats out there.
Bad: you could blow all your pocket money in one fell swoop.

**www.crystalskins.com**
Good: perfect for princesses. If you like bling, this is definitely for you. You send in your mobile, iPod, trainers, etc, and they cover it in crystals.
Bad: very expensive.

**www.ladymissfoofoo.com**
Good: simple site with great accessories, loads of charm bracelets and necklaces.
Bad: the design is drear.

**www.moretvicar.com**
Good: if you want cool T-shirts, this is for you. Fab logos and sayings.
Bad: some sections don't have much choice.

**www.swapitshop.com**
Good: great site for under-18s. It's basically like a teen eBay site where you swap your stuff with others. Good security on here as well. If you're under 16 you can use your mum's or dad's email address so they can monitor what's being swapped.
Bad: you will become completely hooked.

**www.ellegirl.com**
Good: loads of articles and forums. Paradise for any self-confessed fashion lover.
Bad: you will get lost in cyber space.

**www.teenvogue.com**
Good: one of the best teen magazines on the market. You can subscribe for $42.00 including shipping.
Bad: annoying pop-ups.

**www.girlshop.com**
Good: fun American site with great fashion and related items. Things do sell out quite fast.
Bad: shipping from the US so be prepared for that cost.

**www.dubitcard.com**
Good: free discount card for under-18s! There are loads of high street shops that are part of the dubit scheme.
Bad: this could encourage you to spend, spend, spend.

## Making a difference

**www.g-nation.co.uk**
Good: make a difference in the world and give to causes, help set up charities or do some volunteer work. Our planet is changing so why not be aware and join g-nation? It's a really cool site.
Bad: nothing.

**www.princes-trust.org.uk**
Good: amazing organisation that literally transforms young people's lives. The site is really informative, check it out and give yourself a chance.
Bad: the design is a little bit boring, but please don't let that put you off.

**www.do-it.org.uk**
Good: inspirational site if you want to become a volunteer (you need to be 16-29).
Bad: nothing, the world needs people like you!

## Advice/Help

**www.there4me.com**
Good: revolutionary site in association with the NSPCC. Strictly confidential – you can talk to professionals online about your problems. Check out the safety rules.
Bad: nothing.

**www.teentoday.co.uk**
Good: online community dedicated to teenagers.
Bad: could be isolating.

**www.talktofrank.com**
Good: brilliant way to talk about your problems in private. There is a comprehensive section on drugs and where you can get help in your area.
Bad: nothing, a fantastic site.

**www.need2know.co.uk**
Good: great design, lots of interesting articles about love, life and so much more. Being a teenager can have its hardships so tune into this site and get all the support you need.
Bad: not much.

**www.coolnurse.com**
Good: American site purely dedicated to teenagers. If you feel that you can't talk to anybody, this is a great way of discussing your problems.
Bad: it's quite American.

**www.beinggirl.com**
Good: brilliant site for girls, written by girls. The layout is fantastic and really interesting. Great articles as well as really useful tips about your body, relationships and tons more.
Bad: not much, this site is really well thought out.

## Music

**www.itunes.com**
Good: revolutionary way to buy your tunes. Most singles cost 79p. Highly addictive!
Bad: not the greatest selection in the world.

**www.dolphindiscs.com**
Good: if you're looking for unusual music, this is definitely for you.
Bad: rather old school – you can't download directly to your computer.

**www.juno.co.uk**
Good: online music store where you can listen to tunes before buying them. You can also get hold of vinyl from here.
Bad: not much.

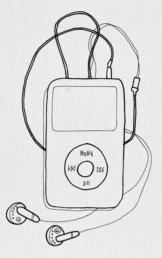

**www.tunetribe.com**
Good: very cool site for real music lovers. They have a seriously good range of music.
Bad: you will end up spending loads of money.

**www.halfinchrecordings.com**
Good: mad bootleg tracks. Only teenagers will get this one.
Bad: very confusing site.

**www.htfr.co.uk**
Good: struggling to find a tune? Check this out, it will save your life.
Bad: the homepage will freak you out...it's full on!

**www.lyrics.com**
Good: genius! Click on any song you like and get the full lyrics.
Bad: too many ads and pop ups.

**www.cd-wow.com**
Good: if you are still into buying CDs, this is a great site, really good value.
Bad: you could be broke quite quickly.

## Gossip

**www.teenhollywood.com**
Good: access all areas with the best scoop on teen Hollywood.
Bad: you will become obsessed.

**www.blissmag.co.uk**
Good: girly heaven! Online magazine with so much gossip and fashion you'll never leave the house.
Bad: too many pop ups.

**www.popworld.com**
Good: loads of pop gossip!
Bad: too many mobile phone adverts, so manipulative. Also the site has a few problems at times.

**www.cosmogirl.co.uk**
Good: great online magazine. Fun articles and silly quizzes.
Bad: annoying flashing ad banners!

**www.glittergirl.co.uk**
Good: fun, girly interactive world. Loads of games and different things to do. Perfect on a rainy day.
Bad: be careful while using the chat rooms as any one can log on.

**www.mykindaplace.com**
Good: teen heaven. So much gossip, games, forums and tons more that you won't get bored.
Bad: you may get lost in cyber-space.

**www.globalgang.org.uk**
Good: fun site for younger teens. Find out what other teenagers get up to all over the world.
Bad: not much.

# travel

## Online booking

### www.ba.com
Good: reliable and safe, this is one of the best sites around. Very easy to use and hassle free.
Bad: not much.

### www.easyjet.com
Good: the pioneer in low-cost travel. So easy to book. You can change you bookings at any time this will cost an extra £20.00 well worth it considering most airlines don't allow this.
Bad: You need to book well in advance for the cheapest deals.

### www.eurostar.com
Good: escape to the world's most romantic city, easy to book online. The most practical way to get to Paris.
Bad: you have to book early to get the cheapest deals.

### www.i-escape.com
Good: amazing travel site with the most fantastic destinations. There are no booking fees. Very refreshing site with original places to go.
Bad: not much, the minute you click on here you'll want to book a holiday.

### www.expedia.com
Good: Great site with loads of options. The best one is the inspirator – click on it answer three questions and it gives you great ideas on where to go.
Bad: You need patience while surfing

### www.lastminute.com
Good: loads of holidays and last-minute deals.
Bad: they never seem to have what you are looking for! The dates rarely match the ones you want.

### www.opodo.co.uk
Good: Great site – the layout alone makes you want to go on holiday. Very good deals. The meaningful travel section is fantastic especially for gap years or if you want to do something that makes a difference, such as working with orang-utans, saving turtles and much much more.
Bad: overwhelming amount of choices!

### www.responsibletravel.com
Good: revolutionary idea to promote responsible travel, make a difference while travelling and do something productive, such as helping the gorillas in Africa etc.
Bad: most trips are quite expensive but you can opt for a budget trip.

### www.tripadvisor.com
Good: Brilliant site reviewed by fellow travellers. Find hotels, flights etc… so much information you can surf on here for hours.
Bad: you can't book flights directly through them, you have to click on other travel sites.

### www.smallfamilies.co.uk
Good: this travel site is totally dedicated to single parents taking

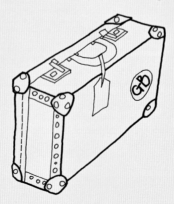

their kids on holiday.
Bad: you have to leave your details and they get back to you, no online bookings.

### www.bargainholidays.com
Good: the best deals for flights to the Caribbean, India and more. They are literally chucking bargain flights at you!
Bad: the dates you want are not always available.

### www.ebookers.com
Good: Simple and clean site. Very efficient, you can find everything you need from flights to hotels.
Bad: not much

### www.babygoes2.com
Good: an entire site dedicated to holidays with your little darlings. They really have thought about everything on here, from the flight duration to the local food, which jabs you may need, what to pack for the kids on long haul flights etc… simply brilliant.
Bad: You could be surfing on this site for hours and hours.

### www.ryanair.com
Good, super cheap flights, the site is easy to use.
Bad: be careful, as they do not go to main airports! Do not expect anything from this airline. Everything costs extra, even a smile – hence the cheapness!

### www.itravel.com
good: brilliant for cheap hotels, this is more of a portal. The links are fantastic.
Bad: too much! From house sales to holidays to dating… where are they going with all this!

## Accommodation

### www.hiphotels.net
Good: finally a site that offers something special when booking a hotel. There are so many sites that offer bog standard accommodation. This is really refreshing!
Bad: sadly not enough choice… just doesn't quite cut it.

### www.couchsurfing.com
Good: A revolutionary way of travelling. Basically you stay on people's couches! An amazing way to make connections worldwide. Read the safety guide as this site really makes people's safety their number one priority.
Bad: a little confusing at first. Persevere and you'll get there.

### www.londontown.com
Good: everything you need to find in London. There is a fantastic selection of hotels and B&Bs, shopping, entertainment and loads more.
Bad: some things are slightly out of date.

### www.hotelguide.com
Good: find any hotel you like on this site, from super deluxe to funky hostels. There is something for everybody.
Bad: sometimes the site doesn't work properly.

### www.corncott.com
Good: this site is purely dedicated to renting cottages in Cornwall. Fairly easy to use, hundreds of cottages to chose from.
Bad: The search can take hours!

### www.bedandbreakfasts-uk.co.uk
Good: out of all the B&B sites this is the most interesting and functional. The B&B selection is fab..
Bad: not much

### www.hostels.com
Good: find a hostel any where in the world, brilliant rating system written by people who have stayed in the hostel you choose. The comments are very honest.
Bad: you have to trust the comments of strangers and could be running the risk of staying in a dump.

### www.telegraph.co.uk/travel
Good: great travel section. Really good for short city breaks with links to hotels.
Bad: you end up surfing for hours!

## Railways

### www.nationalrail.co.uk
Good: all the information you need about train fares and travel. You can get all the information sent to you by text.
Bad: Slightly confusing when it comes to booking online, could be simpler.

### www.tubeplanner.com
Good: so easy to use, just type in your journey and the tube planner will tell you exactly which tube lines to catch.
Bad: not much as this site is so straightforward.

### www.thetube.com
Good: up to the minute info on delays so you can plan your journey. Pay the congestion charge online, full London weather section, cycle routes throughout London. A great site for getting around town.
Bad: the tube route planner is badly designed and confusing to use.

### www.qjump.co.uk
Good: great idea, you can have your tickets delivered on the same day if you book them between 8 am and 3 pm.
Bad: only available in London.

### www.seat61.com
Good: Brilliant site that basically tell you how to get from London to anywhere in the world by train! Links to other rail sites as well on here.
Bad: can be a tad overwhelming when you first log on.

### www.thetrainline.com
Good: Book a train ticket for any where in the world. For UK travel, just type in all the info you have and trainline will find your journey times.
Bad: the site can be a bit tricky to use and you also need to log in.

## Useful travel sites

### www.cybercafes.com
Good: Fantastic site!! Totally vital in this day and age. If you are travelling and need a cyber café, go to this site and they list every country and cyber café available.
Bad: nothing! This site is fabulous.

### www.visaservice.co.uk
Good: Very informative site. Find out every thing you need as far as visas are concerned.
Bad: quite a dull site. But then again finding out about visas isn't going to be enthralling.

### www.ukpa.gov.uk
Good: Passport Office site. You can renew your passport or apply for a new one. All the information you need is on this site. Very well explained.
Bad: not very exciting.

**www.tripprep.com**
Good: this site tells you which vaccines you need for which country. Very good site.
Bad: you have to log in and if your browser doesn't accept cookies, you can't access the site.

**www.thebathroomdiaries.com**
Good: imagine you are in the middle of nowhere, nature calls and you need to find a clean user-friendly loo! This site has the best bathrooms and public loos in over 100 countries.
Bad: Not enough choice!

**www.journeywoman.com**
Good: great site for woman travellers. There are loads of safe places to stay worldwide – a real female community on this site.
Bad: not much!

**www.guardian.co.uk/travel**
Good: what a fab site! Everything you need to know about travelling and where to go. The 'been there' section gives you first-hand experience of fellow travellers and there are views on various places. Also, there are really good links to other travel sites.
Bad: you can get side-tracked as there is so much to look at.

**www.busabout.com**
Good: travel across Europe on buses! Very comprehensive guide around cities with maps and loads of info.
Bad: you must book early to avoid disappointment.

**www.lonelyplanet.com**
Good: excellent travel guide once you figure out how to work this site.
Bad: confusing!! At times the site does not work properly.

**www.traintaxi.co.uk**
Good: vital site! All you need to know about the taxi situation at any railway station across Britain. They have phone numbers for local taxi services in smaller towns where it may be harder to find a cab! The site is constantly updated.
Bad: nothing at all.

**www.timeout.com**
Good: loads of good information on various cities worldwide. From clubs to theatre and loads more. Most bookings are linked to the major travel sites, easy to use.
Bad: the home page is rather full on and can be daunting at first.

## Car hire

**www.easycar.com**
Good: straightforward site and easy to use – just type in your information.
Bad: most cars are pretty basic: you won't be renting any beauties from here.

**www.hertz.com**
Good: rent a car anywhere in the world with hertz. They have a wide choice of cars.
Bad: not the easiest site, slightly confusing.

**www.avis.co.uk**
Good: great site with a great choice of cars. Check out the prestige section to book luxurious cars. Booking could not be any easier!
Bad: not all countries supply luxury cars.

# useful directories

**www.google.co.uk**
Good: probably the best search engine around. Check out our guide to Googling for more information.
Bad: not much! This has revolutionised life on the internet.

**www.ask.com**
Good: another fantastic search engine, slightly more personal than Google. There are a lot of brilliant options on here as well.
Bad: nothing.

**www.urbanpa.com**
Good: great idea – if you are too busy and need someone to help you sort your home, paperwork, etc, then book an urban personal assistant to run your errands and do odd jobs.
Bad: it's expensive.

**www.fulltimemothers.org**
Good: a site dedicated to stay-at-home mums. There are very good links to other related sites and you can chat to other mums online.
Bad: the design is awful!

**www.netmums.com**
Good: fabulous site for mums by mums! Everything you need to know from where the best local schools are to moving house.
Bad: an awful lot of information to get through!

**www.womenatwork.co.uk**
Good: an entire directory of women who run small businesses. So if you are freelance, you can advertise your business here.
Bad: you have to register and pay a fee.

**www.mothers35plus.co.uk**
Good: especially designed for 'older mothers', this has great tips and information as well as chat rooms.
Bad: not much – this is a really well thought-out site.

**www.appealnow.com**
Good: appeal against parking tickets, clamping, etc. You simply contest the fine and they do the rest for you.
Bad: it can take several weeks for the appeal to go through.

**www.hintsandthings.co.uk**
Good: loads of brilliant tips on everything to do with your home, garden and pets. Check out the health and beauty tips as well – there are some really bizarre things to be found.
Bad: the design may put you off.

**www.crimereduction.co.uk**
Good: everything you need to know about the crime rate in your area and what you can do to help.
Bad: rather depressing.

**www.which.co.uk**
Good: expert advice on loads of different issues.
Bad: an awful lot of reading is required.

**www.ipodhacks.com**
Good: everything you need to know to use your iPod to its full potential.
Bad: obsessive making.

**www.yell.com**
Good: online yellow pages. Type in what you're looking for and get the number for free.
Bad: nothing, it's great to get a free service!

**www.disability.gov.uk**
Good: fantastic directory with loads of information and useful links.
Bad: nothing.

**www.direct.gov.uk**
Good: everything you need to know about the government and related issues.
Bad: so much stuff.

**www.writetothem.com**
Good: got a burning question for your MP? Get your voice heard and write to them.
Bad: nothing.

**www.driveuhome.co.uk**
Good: if you have had one too many and can't drive home, book a driver. They come on a fold-up bike and drive you and your car home safely.
Bad: London area only.

**www.drugs.gov.uk**
Good: all the information you need to know about drugs, treatment and intervention. Vital site.
Bad: not much, although there is an awful lot to read.

**www.givingupsmoking.co.uk**
Good: an entire portal dedicated to giving up smoking with brilliant links available.
Bad: it's the hardest thing to give up, but hopefully this will help.

**www.samaritans.co.uk**
Good: simple and easy lifeline site – simply email them and someone will get back to you.
Bad: nothing.

**www.bullying.co.uk**
Good: absolutely brilliant site to help people who are being bullied. There is a safe online chat room. Very straightforward and easy to use.
Bad: nothing.

# weird & wonderful

**www.mulletsgalore.com**
Pure mullet heaven. Some of the photos are out of this world… seriously mad hairdos.

**www.mugshots.com**
Mad site dedicated to mug shots! From the Most Wanted to some people you may recognise.

**www.freakingnews.com**
Bizarre site with funny pictures on strange news items. True or false…you decide.

**www.officeolympics.com**
If you're bored at work, then this site is hilarious – you can play office Olympics with your chairs!

**www.iusedtobelieve.com**
Fantastic site dedicated to all those strange things you used to believe in as a child. You can get lost in this site for hours as some of the beliefs are truly hilarious. You can also send in your own stories.

**www.nicecupofteaandasit-down.com**
Everything you need to know about how to sit down and have a nice cup of tea. Check out the best biscuits as voted by you.

**www.thisistrue.com**
From the weird to the utterly bizarre, this site is full of strange but true stories.

**www.footballanorak.com**
If you want to know all the statistics on premiership players, i.e. how many goals has Henry scored this season… this will be your dream site.

**www.streakerama.com**
Find out everything you need to know about streakers and why they do it!

**www.thefaceanalyzer.com**
Download a picture of yourself and the face analyzer will tell you all about yourself… sounds fun but it's rather complicated to use!

**www.engrish.com**
Funny site that points out English mistakes made in Japanese advertising. There are some true gems on here!

**www.whitehouse.org**
Very funny site that takes the mickey out of the White House!

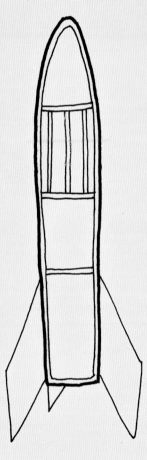

**www.snapbubbles.com**
If you are really bored or simply love bubble wrap, this site was made for you, You just snap bubbles with your mouse.

**www.uglydress.com**
Some of the worst bridesmaids' dresses and so many more items of clothing can be seen on this genius web site

**www.borgstrom.com**
With the help of your mouse you slap the man with the beard! Mad site that is great entertainment if you are really bored!

**www.emotioneric.com**
At first you may look at this and not really find it funny, but as you see more pictures you may actually catch yourself laughing out loud.

**www.pickthehottie.com**
Hilariously weird site. Basically pick who you think is hot! It can be cruel as you could post a photo of someone you dislike and they get voted on by the world!

**www.snopes.com**
Pure genius – all about urban myths. You can spend hours on here.

**www.badfads.com**
Some of the worst fashion crimes of the last century, from bouffant hair to cat suits. You'll have such a giggle with this site.

**www.20q.net**
This is a brilliant site if you are bored at work and fancy a quick distraction.
You think of a subject and play 20 questions. Most the time they guess your answer!

**www.smalltime.com/dictator**
This is beyond freaky...you think of a soap character (American mainly) and then you answer loads of questions and the computer guesses who you are.

**www.optillusions.com**
Loads of fab optical illusions on this site, there are some amazing ones that you can download. The flashy banners may drive you crazy.

**www.uglyfootballers.com**
Check this out: you can go back to the eighties and seventies when it was all mullets and sideburns. Look at the ugly hall of fame.

**www.rocketguy.com**
This guy is planning to shoot himself into the atmosphere! A site well worth checking out on a rainy day.

**www.marsnews.com**
Find out if there is life on Mars...loads of articles and pictures of the red planet. Spooky.

**www.mreclipse.com**
If you don't want to miss out on the next total eclipse, this site will give you all the information you need to know.

**www.hellsgeriatrics.com**
A site dedicated to the over-fifties: their motto is 'grow old disgracefully'! Full of funny stories and loads of great features.

**www.lazystudent.co.uk/rejectline.html**
Not brave enough to reject someone? Log on to this site. Very funny indeed! Let others do your dirty work...ouch!

**www.cockneyrhymingslang.co.uk**
Learn the true meaning of cockney rhyming slang. There is an A–Z list on every word under the sun. You could get obsessed on here.

**www.islandsforsale.com**
Sick and tired of living in the fast lane? Why not think about buying your own island...it's good to dream.

**www.spinon.co.uk**
Genius site where you can play interactive games against politicians – such as throwing eggs at them and loads more!

**www.mrwinkle.com**
Strange site dedicated to the fluffiest little dog...pretty pointless but very entertaining.

**www.antwrp.gsfc.nasa.gov/apod**
Discover the cosmos with a different amazing picture of the universe every day. There is a list of photos from 1995 to now!

Illustrations by Joanna Cannon
www.joannacannon.com

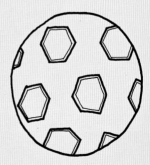

# Index

# Acknowledgements

To all the mums below who juggle career and kids and continue to be an  inspiration to us and everyone who knows them
Adela Campbell
Booney Henriques
Dany Cox
Emma Askari
Emma Hardy
Melanie Metcalf
Pia Marocco
Sophie Montgomery
Susie Forbes

...and to enthusiastic shopper
Romilly McAlpine

...and to those who keep us healthy, happy, sane and on top of the ageing process:
Dr Jean-Louis Sebagh
Dr Diana Mariton MD
Mr Peter Butler, MD, FRCSI, FRCS(Eng), FRCS(Plast)
Roberta Stimson
Dr Nonna Brenner
Bernadette Carey

...and to the professionals
The British Red Cross
Cancer Research UK

...and to our working family who make everything possible and put up with our chaos:
**Antonia da Silva** – for sticking with the hardest job in the world
**Azusana Gruz** – for her unique tailoring
**Caroline Baker** – for being the most organized saint in the world
**Charlotte Ribeyro** – more than just a make-up artist
**Clive Hayball** – for understanding us
**Cristiano Basciu** – the biggest drama queen in the team
**David Rowley** – for his design genius
**Henry Golding** – for being so handsome and straight
**Jacinta Silva** – for putting up with the Bertelsen brood
**Jenny Kensett** – for being there always
**Jessica Jones** – for being born
**Jinny Johnson** – for checking text
**Justin Hunt** – for design and photography support
**Leander Fairey** – who will go beyond the call of duty always smiling
**Liberty Frazer** – for dealing with chaos calmly
**Lucy, Chantal and Emma** – the real hard workers
**Margaret Langton** – for her dependability
**Martine de Rocles** – Merci pour tous
**Melanie Lewis** – for always smiling
**Michael Foster** – for being himself
**Robin Matthews** – for his calm and creativity
**Sacha Mavroleon** – our mascot and much more
**Sue Spick** – for always being there
**Susan Haynes** – for looking better every year we work with her
**Zoe Lem** – for being such a wonderful pupil

...and, most importantly, our husbands and children, for whom we do it all

TO JESSICA
For all her blood, sweat and tears

First published in Great Britain in 2006
by Weidenfeld & Nicolson

This paperback edition first published in 2007
by Weidenfeld & Nicolson
10 9 8 7 6 5 4 3 2 1

A CIP catalogue record for this book is available from the British Library.
isbn-13: 978 0 297 85346 6
isbn-10: 0 297 84426 1

The Orion Publishing Group's policy is to use papers that are natural,
renewable and recyclable products and made from wood grown in
sustainable forests. The logging and manufacturing processes are expected
to conform to the environmental regulations of the country of origin.

Design and art direction by David Rowley
Editorial director Susan Haynes
Design by Clive Hayball and Lippa Pearce
Assisted by Justin Hunt
Handwritten fonts and chapter openers by Marion Deuchars
Edited by Jinny Johnson
Index by Elizabeth Wiggans

Printed in Italy

Weidenfeld & Nicolson
The Orion Publishing Group Ltd
Orion House
5 Upper St Martin's Lane
London WC2H 9EA
www.orionbooks.co.uk